Colli...on

Grade Booster

Maths
Foundation

Rosie... ...hes

Contents

Introduction

About this Book

This book has been designed to support your preparation for the foundation tier Edexcel GCSE mathematics exam papers. There are sections with advice and ideas about how to revise, what you need to know and ways to learn it. Other chapters contain examples, split by topic, to give you an idea of what some of the trickier exam questions might look like and what good answers to those questions would be.

The non-calculator symbol 🖩 appears beside questions that you are expected to be able to answer without a calculator. You should remember that a similar question could still appear on a calculator paper. When attempting these questions, try them without a calculator. It can be easy to make calculation errors, so it is important to practise even if it seems a relatively easy step in the question.

This book aims to help you to apply the knowledge you already have in your 'mathematical toolbox'. It focuses on how to implement the skills you already have in a variety of contexts.

Students often lose marks through misconceptions, feeling lost when a question is unfamiliar or making silly mistakes. This book aims to highlight ways to get started, build confidence, spot possible misconceptions and show ways of checking your working as you go.

There are many different ways to approach mathematical problems. It is worth having a go at each example question yourself before looking through the answer – it may be that you have an even more concise way of doing it, or a method that makes more sense to you. Different approaches are fine as long as you obey mathematical logic and show clearly what steps you have taken. Answers should be the same whatever method you use. You can work through the examples in order or dip in and out, whatever your preference. The examples have hints and tips alongside them. The symbol ✓ helps to show where individual marks would be awarded in the workings and answers.

Questions on the exam papers can be expected to be worth up to 6 marks. However, to get the most out of the examples, some questions in this book are allocated more than 6 marks. Any aspect of these examples could represent part of an exam question, but you wouldn't necessarily expect to see them all included in one single question.

At the end of each chapter, you are signposted to pages in the *Collins Edexcel Maths Foundation Revision Guide* (ISBN 9780008112615) for more information on the topics covered. The same page references apply to the *Collins Edexcel Maths Foundation All-in-One Revision & Practice* book (ISBN 9780008112493).

Terms in **bold** are among those defined in the Glossary at the back of the book.

The Edexcel GCSE (9–1) Course

The syllabus has been developed with the aim of increasing your ability to transfer skills between topics, school subjects and on into higher education or work. You will need to apply a mixture of mathematical skills in new situations and to solve problems. There is a focus on your ability to reason mathematically, both to draw conclusions and to consider accuracy within the work you are doing. The ability to communicate clearly and concisely is also important. You are expected to have a good grasp of key conventions and mathematical notation so that your work can be understood universally. Understanding is key and, as there are generally many ways to answer the questions you will be asked, your ability to show your understanding and explain your method becomes all the more important.

The Exams

- You will sit <u>three exam papers</u>. The first paper is a non-calculator paper, testing your mental and written methods alongside particular topic knowledge. The other two are calculator papers, allowing more focus on the context and strategies, rather than the 'number crunching'. All topics studied can appear on any of the three papers.
- <u>Each paper has 80 marks and lasts 1 hour and 30 minutes.</u> When practising exam questions, this works out at roughly 1 mark a minute.
- There are two tiers of entry – higher (grades 4 to 9) and foundation (grades 1 to 5). This book supports the foundation tier specification. The three papers that you will sit all have to be from the same tier and be taken in the same exam series. That means you will be sitting three foundation tier papers, either in the summer or possibly (if you are resitting and over 16 years of age) in November.

Foundation Tier Topic Overview

The topics will be assessed based on the following weightings:

Topic	Weighting
Number (see Chapter 3)	25%
Ratio, Proportion and Rates of Change (see Chapter 5)	25%
Algebra (see Chapter 4)	20%
Geometry and Measures (see Chapter 6)	15%
Probability and Statistics (see Chapters 7 and 8)	15%

Assessment Objectives Overview

The style of questions are categorised in the following way:

Assessment Objective and Weighting	Requirements
AO1 Use and apply standard techniques 50%	• Accurately recall facts, terminology and definitions • Use and interpret notation correctly • Accurately carry out routine procedures • Accurately carry out set tasks requiring multi-step solutions
AO2 Reason, interpret and communicate mathematically 25%	• Make deductions and inferences to draw conclusions from mathematical information • Construct chains of reasoning to achieve a given result • Interpret and communicate information accurately • Present arguments and proofs • Assess the validity of an argument and critically evaluate a given way of presenting information
AO3 Solve problems within mathematics and in other contexts 25%	• Translate problems in mathematical or non-mathematical contexts into a process or a series of mathematical processes • Make and use connections between different parts of mathematics • Interpret results in the context of the given problem • Evaluate methods used and results obtained • Evaluate solutions to identify how they may have been affected by assumptions made

The different types of question give you the opportunity to show that you can:
• remember key facts and use them to solve a problem
• solve problems by making use of your mathematical knowledge in less familiar situations.

This book mainly focuses on the AO2 and AO3 styles of questions.

See Chapter 9 for examples, hints, tips and methods for dealing with the different types of questions.

2   Learning and Revising Mathematics

> *"Luck is not chance–*
> *It's Toil–*
> *Fortune's expensive smile*
> *Is earned–"*
>
> — Emily Dickinson

Mathematics is a skills-based subject so the most useful way to prepare is to practise, practise, practise. There are some knowledge-based elements, formulae and facts you need to remember. More detail about what you 'need to know' can be found in Chapter 10.

Planning Your Revision

However much time you have left before your exam, there is always a lot that you can do. Think carefully about what you are doing and how you are doing it.

Long-term Preparation

The key with maths is making sure you understand everything as it is taught, and then revisiting topics regularly, especially ones you find challenging. Think about building in a regular slot to look over past topics. Make notes and refine those notes as you go. Doing small amounts of regular work means that there is less need for cramming, and stress, when it comes to an exam.

Shorter-term Preparation

If you have relatively limited time left, make sure you plan how to use that time most efficiently (do not spend too long planning though). It can be tempting to work on a topic that makes you feel good because you can do it. However, in terms of adding marks to your exam performance, it is likely to mean a lot of time for perhaps only a few extra marks. Instead, pick out topics that you know you struggle with, find different ways to work on them and feel good when you conquer something that you started out dreading.

Be Organised

Whether you are someone who is naturally organised or chaotic, it is worth putting in place a structure to help you keep on top of what you are doing, for example:
- Lists of topics that you can tick off for showing you have learned/reviewed/are confident in. Colour coding can work well.
- A record of which past papers you have already done, how you did and what specific things you need to improve.

Your teacher might be able to provide you with a template for these or you might need to do some research yourself.

Create Time and Space

In order to focus on your work, give yourself a positive environment to work in. A quiet space where you are unlikely to be interrupted is a good start. Turn off your phone and the television. You might think you can multi-task, but give your brain a chance to focus. Make it comfortable – working on a desk gives you much better posture and can help you to concentrate.

Be Kind to Yourself

In the run-up to exams it can be easy to intend to dedicate every last minute to revision but then get distracted and put it off. This cycle can make you feel guilty and overwhelmed. To help you work hard and remain focused, plan to take breaks and take them guilt-free (as long as there aren't too many and they aren't too long!). Your brain needs some downtime to process the information you have been revising.

A good revision plan allows some overflow sessions. These can be used to do a bit extra on something you run out of time for, without disrupting the rest of the plan. If you had time for everything, you can then have a bonus session off. Try to be realistic about what you can achieve in a one-hour or two-hour session.

Eat, Drink, Sleep and Exercise

Give your body and your brain what it needs to function at the top level.

Enjoy It

This may sound ridiculous, or completely obvious to you, but problem-solving and logic puzzles can be really rewarding and enjoyable, as shown by the popularity of number puzzles like Sudoku. Sometimes it is hard to enjoy the process because you are so focused on the final goal. Enjoy each question and activity for what it is. Don't panic! When you get stuck, it is a chance for you to solve something really tricky, which is far more rewarding than doing something that comes easily to you.

Practise, Practise, Practise

Maths is a skill in applying logic and problem-solving. The best way to improve is to practise, and practise regularly. Practising maths isn't just about working through piles of past exam questions, though that should be part of it:

Exam-style questions	It is important to be aware of how questions are likely to look in an exam so that it isn't too confusing when you open your paper.
Puzzles and activities	In lessons you are likely to have come across a mixture of activities to develop understanding of different topics. Consider using these in your own revision. You might want to make something yourself, ask a teacher or find something from a website.
What else?	Ask yourself what else a question could ask. If there was an extra part, what might it ask? If you were writing this exam paper, how might you make this question harder? This will allow you to get even more out of every question.
Spot the 'tricks'	Examiners don't set out to trick you but exam questions will include elements that are likely to trip up candidates. Spend time reading through questions and thinking about what might be the thing that would catch out candidates. Spotting what makes a question harder is a great way of planning how to get around the difficulty.
Calculators	Being familiar with your calculator is very important (whether it is your personal one or a school one). Take it to all your lessons and make sure you can use it efficiently and effectively. Always question your calculator; if your calculator suggests a door is 30 m tall, it may be worth double checking. There is a risk that you trust your calculator more than your common sense – the calculator will give you the correct answer to what you input but it is easy to make mistakes in the process. Your method is still very important so write down any calculations you do with your calculator, not just the answer.
Non-calculator questions	Don't be tempted to use a calculator when practising a non-calculator question. It is easy to decide to save time by bypassing the time-consuming process of carrying out written calculations, especially if a calculator is sitting right there. Calculation errors and silly mistakes are very common. By focusing on and practising calculations, even when they seem easy, you are more likely to spot mistakes and reduce errors. Marks will be awarded for method, so you should get used to showing clearly what you are doing.
Check your answers	Don't reach for the answer booklet too soon. Try putting in some self-checking processes and seeing if you can find any mistakes yourself.

How to Learn Things

Different people's memories work in different ways. Here are some ideas of how to help you memorise the information that you need, given that developing a photographic memory is unlikely:

Prove it / understand it	Understanding where a fact or **formula** comes from means that, rather than just remembering the formation of letters, you know why it appears the way it does. This might also help you work out the fact or formula even if you cannot remember it. For example, many students lose marks by misremembering the laws of indices. If you know that there is a rule to answer $a^{12} \times a^5$, think about what an index means. Consider a simple case, like $a^2 \times a^3 = a \times a \times a \times a \times a = a^5$, to confirm that you need to add the powers. $a^{12} \times a^5 = a^{17}$
Make a link	Making a link might be a mnemonic to remember SOH CAH TOA (Some Old Horse Caught Another Horse Taking Oats Away) or a formula. For example, speed can be measured in miles per hour (something you should already know so do not need to learn): miles measure distance, hour is time and 'per' means divide, so Speed $= \frac{\text{Distance}}{\text{Time}}$
Write it out	To help something stick, writing it out can help as it connects with your muscle memory. In turn, this gives your brain an extra connection.
Create flashcards	Double-sided cards are easy to carry around and handy for testing yourself and your friends. They are useful for formulae but also for things like recognising key features of numbers.
Do something active	Walk the lines in an angles question, turning through the angles. Some people's brains really thrive by linking a physical movement with the fact.
Do something peculiar	The more links you can make the better. If you can connect a funny or odd event or activity with a fact that you have to learn, it gives your brain more cross-references with which to unlock the information.
Make posters	By making a poster you will consider the topic, what goes together and what similarities and differences there are. You might link visual images with an **equation** or value. All of this creates useful connections which help your brain to cross reference, store and find information when you need it.
Use your posters	Put up your posters somewhere you will see them often. Consider moving the posters around every now and then so they don't start blending into the background.
Use it	As part of your practice, you will use your store of knowledge, which in turn will help you to remember it. Think about ways to test yourself. It can be easy to think you know everything if it is written down next to you as you work and, whilst it will be filtering in slowly, there are things you can do alongside the questions to boost your uptake: • Work without any formulae and note down the ones you had to look up; use the formulae for a poster, copy them out a few times and stick them on notes by your bed. Ensure that you won't need to look them up next time. • Make a lift-the-flap formulae guide, letting you see what formulae there are available to you without giving them away. You can also add a hint flap to help build in a connection.

Luck is 95% hard work and 5% good fortune... nevertheless – GOOD LUCK!

Number

Good numeracy skills underpin nearly every part of mathematics. Number takes the study of numbers a step further. Topics at GCSE look at how you are able to manipulate, interpret and express numbers in order to solve a range of problems.

3.1 Comparing Numbers

You need to be able to compare numbers in their different forms. Marks are often dropped in these questions, so take your time and make sure you get the ascending/descending order correct.

Example 3.1

a) Write the following numbers in ascending order:

0.0041, 0.04, 0.004, 0.0104, 0.00414 *(2 marks)*

0.00410

0.04000

0.00400

0.01040

0.00414

Ascending, smallest to largest:

0.004, 0.0041, 0.00414, 0.0104, 0.04 ✓ ✓

> Ascending means increasing in value. If you are comparing decimals, consider writing them under each other lined up by the decimal point. You can also write in zeros so that they all have the same number of decimal places.

b) Write the following numbers in descending order:

$\frac{1}{2}, \frac{3}{4}, \frac{8}{24}, \frac{2}{3}, \frac{5}{12}$ *(3 marks)*

All can be converted to twelfths:

$\frac{6}{12}, \frac{9}{12}, \frac{4}{12}, \frac{8}{12}, \frac{5}{12}$ ✓

③ ① ⑤ ② ④

$\frac{3}{4}, \frac{2}{3}, \frac{1}{2}, \frac{5}{12}, \frac{8}{24}$ ✓ ✓

$\frac{1}{2} = \frac{6}{12}$ (×6)

$\frac{8}{24} = \frac{4}{12}$ (÷2)

$\frac{3}{4} = \frac{9}{12}$ (×3)

$\frac{2}{3} = \frac{8}{12}$ (×4)

> Fractions are easy to compare if they have the same denominator, so find the equivalent fractions. If you cannot spot a common denominator, you can use other methods (e.g. converting into decimals).

c) Write the following numbers in ascending order:

0.15, –0.23, –0.02, 0.02, –0.19, –0.189   (*3 marks*)

Negatives can cause confusion. Think about a number line: the 'bigger' negative numbers have less value than the 'smaller' ones. For example, –10 < –2 and in context –10°C is colder than –2°C.

–0.23, –0.19, –0.189, –0.02, 0.02, 0.15 ✓ ✓ ✓ | Consider the negatives and positives in two separate groups if needed.

3.2 Converting Numbers to Compare

You need to be able to convert values to compare them. This type of question can be given as a set of numbers in different forms for you to list in a certain order or can be given a context. Your main aim is to convert them into a form that enables you to compare them easily.

You can compare numbers in various ways. Decimals will always give an easy comparison once found. Converting to decimals tends to be relatively straightforward too. If you need to use extra written methods to do the calculations, there should be plenty of space to do them. Never feel you should be able to do something in your head, especially as in exam conditions your ability to do mental maths can be put under extra pressure.

Example 3.2

List the following values in ascending order:

46.5, $\frac{5}{7}$ of 63, 12.5% of 368, $\frac{937}{20}$, $45\frac{7}{25}$ (*4 marks*)

Finding values as decimals:

46.5	$\frac{5}{7}$ of 63	12.5% of 368	$\frac{937}{20}$	$45\frac{7}{25}$	
46.5	= (63 ÷ 7) × 5 = (9) × 5 = **45**	10% of 368 = 36.8 5% of 368 = 18.4 2.5% of 368 = 9.2 12.5% of 368 = 36.8 + 9.2 = **46**	= (937 ÷ 2) ÷ 10 = (450 + 15 + 3.5) ÷ 10 = 468.5 ÷ 10 = **46.85**	= 45 + 7 ÷ 25 = 45 + 7 × 4 ÷ 100 = 45 + 28 ÷ 100 = 45 + 0.28 = **45.28**	✓ ✓ ✓
4	Smallest (1)	3	5	2	

Values in <u>ascending</u> order:

$\frac{5}{7}$ of 63, $45\frac{7}{25}$,   12.5% of 368,   46.5, $\frac{937}{20}$ ✓ | The final answer should have the numbers in their original form. Make sure your list is in the right order.

3.3 Systematic Listing Strategies and Types of Number

You need to be able to apply systems for sorting and organising. This can be done in different ways and your chosen method might change depending on the context of the question. It is good to have a method and a way to check wherever possible.

Example 3.3 📱

Lisa has a set of cards:

a) Lisa says that it is a set of **prime numbers.** Is she correct? Justify your answer. *(1 mark)*

Lisa is not correct. 9 is not a prime number as it has factors 1, 3, and 9. ✓

To get this mark, you need to make sure you explain why. You need to refer to the definition of prime numbers and explain why 9 is not prime to justify the answer. Note that 2 is a prime number but it is the only even prime number (as all other even numbers have a **factor** of 2).

b) Lisa takes three cards from the original set and gets:

She uses them to make different three-digit numbers.

i) How many different three-digit numbers can Lisa make? *(2 marks)*

List of numbers Lisa can make:

753   573   375 ✓

735   537   357 ✓

Lisa can make six different three-digit numbers.

ii) What is the biggest difference between two of Lisa's three-digit numbers? *(2 marks)*

Largest 753

Smallest 357 ✓

Difference 753 − 357 = <u>396</u> ✓

$$\begin{array}{r} {}^{6}\cancel{7}{}^{14}\cancel{5}{}^{1}3 \\ -\ 357 \\ \hline \underline{396} \end{array}$$

Remember there are method marks so don't just write a number. Show your working and use some words to make it clear.

3.4 The Four Operations and Different Types of Number

Operations are the things you do to a number or a pair of numbers. The four main operations are adding, subtracting, multiplying and dividing.

The four operations and number types will form part of questions asked across different topics. Negative numbers and fractions often cause problems, and it is an easy way to drop marks unnecessarily. When you spot negatives or fractions, take it slowly and give it the time it deserves. If this is an area of weakness, practise it until it is a strength.

Example 3.4

Answer the following:

a) Calculate $\frac{-7 + 3}{2}$ *(1 mark)*

$$\frac{-7 + 3}{2} = \frac{-4}{2} = -2 \checkmark$$

b) Bob says that the answer to the following calculation is even. Is he correct? Explain how you know.
$4 \times -7 + 2 \times 3 - 6 \times -2$ *(2 marks)*

As each multiplication will give an even answer, the answer to the full calculation will be even (as an even + an even is still even). $\checkmark$
Bob is correct. $\checkmark$

Alternative answer:

$4 \times -7 + 2 \times 3 - 6 \times -2 = -28 + 6 - -12$
$= -22 + 12 - -10 \checkmark$

-10 is an even number so Bob is correct. $\checkmark$

c) Calculate $\frac{1}{2} \div \frac{3}{5} + \frac{2}{9}$, giving your answer as a mixed number. *(3 marks)*

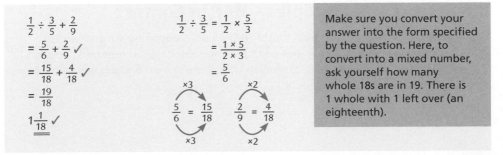

$$\frac{1}{2} \div \frac{3}{5} + \frac{2}{9}$$
$$= \frac{5}{6} + \frac{2}{9} \checkmark$$
$$= \frac{15}{18} + \frac{4}{18} \checkmark$$
$$= \frac{19}{18}$$
$$1\frac{1}{18} \checkmark$$

$$\frac{1}{2} \div \frac{3}{5} = \frac{1}{2} \times \frac{5}{3}$$
$$= \frac{1 \times 5}{2 \times 3}$$
$$= \frac{5}{6}$$

$\frac{5}{6} = \frac{15}{18}$ (×3) $\frac{2}{9} = \frac{4}{18}$ (×2)

Make sure you convert your answer into the form specified by the question. Here, to convert into a mixed number, ask yourself how many whole 18s are in 19. There is 1 whole with 1 left over (an eighteenth).

3.5 Factors and Multiples – LCM in Context

Questions looking for the lowest common multiple (LCM) will often be given in context and will therefore ask for something like 'the least number of packets' or the first time something happens.

Example 3.5 🖩

Two buses, the 590 and the 592, do a circular route through Barton. The 590 completes a loop every 20 minutes. The 592 completes a loop every 45 minutes. Both the 590 and the 592 leave Barton at 8 am.

a) When is the next time both buses will be in Barton together? *(2 marks)*

590 : 08:00, 08:20, 08:40, 09:00, 09:20,
    09:40, 10:00, 10:20, 10:40, 11:00, ...

592 : 08:00, 08:45, 09:30, 10:15, 11:00,
    11:45, 12:30, ... ✓

The next time both buses will be in Barton is 11 am. ✓

> There are other methods for finding the LCM. This example involves listing the multiples and comparing lists.

b) One morning, the 590 is delayed in setting off by 10 minutes.

Will the buses still meet up in Barton? Justify your answer. *(2 marks)*

Times that the 590 is leaving Barton are:
08:10, 08:30, 08:50, 09:10, 09:30, ...

Times that the 592 is leaving Barton are:
08:00, 08:45, 09:30, ... ✓

The buses will meet again at 09:30, then every 3 hours through the day from then on. ✓

3.6 Factors and Multiples – HCF in Context

When finding the highest common factor (HCF), you are looking for the largest number that divides a whole number of times into your original numbers. You might be asked how many people there are when things are shared equally between them, or how many bags should be bought.

Example 3.6

1.4 m

1.12 m

4.2 m

A company stores ice-cream in tubs that are cubes so they fit perfectly into large, rectangular chest freezers as shown.

What is the largest size that these cubes could be and how many would fit into the freezer at that size? *(4 marks)*

Freezer has dimensions 112 cm, 140 cm and 420 cm.

Prime factor decomposition:

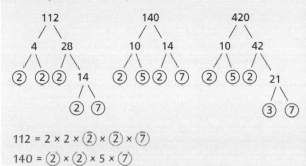

$112 = 2 \times 2 \times 2 \times 2 \times 7$

$140 = 2 \times 2 \times 5 \times 7$

$420 = 2 \times 2 \times 3 \times 5 \times 7$ ✓

The highest common factor is $2 \times 2 \times 7 = 28$ cm

The cubes could measure 28 cm in each dimension. ✓

In the freezer they would be arranged 4 deep by 5 high by 15 along. ✓

$4 \times 5 \times 15 = 300$ ✓

They could fit 300 tubs into the freezer at this size.

As the side length of the cubes must be a factor of all the dimensions of the freezer, you need to find the HCF of 1.12, 1.4 and 4.2. HCF works for integers only, so the first step is to convert the dimensions into cm.

It is good practice to place the factors in ascending order. That way it is easier to compare lists. Identify the prime factors that are 'in common', i.e. the ones that appear for all three numbers.

3.7 Prime Factors and Unique-Prime-Factorisation Theorem

Prime numbers are hugely important and it is worth learning the **prime factors** under 30 so that you recognise them. Unique-prime-factorisation theorem is a fancy name for the idea that all integers (whole numbers) can be broken down into their prime factors, and this prime factor form is unique to the original number. So if the prime factorisation of 55 is 5×11, then no other number in prime factor form will be 5×11 or, for that matter, 11×5. This also means that $5 \times 11 = 11 \times 5 = 55$.

Example 3.7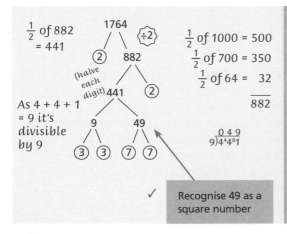

Kaynat says that all the following numbers are different to each other. Drea says that two of them are the same and the odd one out is special because it is a square number.

Number A = $2^2 \times 3 \times 5^2 \times 13$

Number B = $2 \times 3^3 \times 5^2 \times 2 \times 3$

Number C = $3 \times 13 \times 2 \times 5^2 \times 2$

> To compare numbers, it is important to write them in the same form. You can choose to use **powers** (indices) or write each out as a product of prime factors more fully.

a) Show that Drea is right and Kaynat is wrong. *(4 marks)*

A ≠ B

C = $2 \times 2 \times 3 \times 5^2 \times 13$

   = $2^2 \times 3 \times 5^2 \times 13$ ✓

So A = C, so Kaynat is wrong. ✓

B = $2 \times 3^3 \times 5^2 \times 2 \times 3$

   = $2^2 \times 3^4 \times 5^2$

   = $(2 \times 3^2 \times 5) \times (2 \times 3^2 \times 5)$

   = $(2 \times 3^2 \times 5)^2$ ✓

So B is a square number.

As A = C and B is a square number, Drea is right. ✓

> It is possible to compare these numbers by multiplying them out to get A = 3900, B = 8100 and C = 3900. However, as they are all already broken up into prime factor form, it saves time and effort and avoids mistakes to compare them as they are.

> To show that B is a square number, you can show that the prime factors can be divided into two equal groups. If all the powers (indices) are even, then the number is a square number.
> By the same logic, a cube number would have all its powers (indices) divisible by 3. For example, $2^6 \times 3^3 \times 5^3$ is a cube number with a cube root of $2^2 \times 3^1 \times 5^1 = 60$.

b) Use prime factor decomposition to find the **square root** of 1764. *(4 marks)*

$\frac{1}{2}$ of 882 = 441

1764 (÷2)

(halve each digit)

As 4 + 4 + 1 = 9 it's divisible by 9

$\frac{1}{2}$ of 1000 = 500
$\frac{1}{2}$ of 700 = 350
$\frac{1}{2}$ of 64 = 32
_____
882

$9)\overline{4^44^81}$
  049

✓ Recognise 49 as a square number

> When carrying out prime factor decomposition, a factor tree is a good diagram. Look for the obvious factors first. If it is an even number, divide by 2; if it ends in a 5 or 0, divide by 5. 441 is tricky but the examiners are only going to expect you to divide by relatively simple prime numbers on a non-calculator paper. So start by considering 3, 7, 11 and 13. The example uses the fact that if the digits add up to a multiple of 9, then the number will divide by 9. Note that 9 is not a prime number, so the branch doesn't stop there.

$$1764 = 2^2 \times 3^2 \times 7^2 \checkmark$$
$$= (2 \times 3 \times 7)^2$$
$$\sqrt{1764} = 2 \times 3 \times 7 \checkmark$$
$$= 6 \times 7$$
$$= 42$$

The square root of 1764 is 42. $\checkmark$

3.8 Order of Operations

So that mathematical communication is clear, there is a set order in which calculations are carried out. This is often taught with the letters **BIDMAS** or BODMAS.

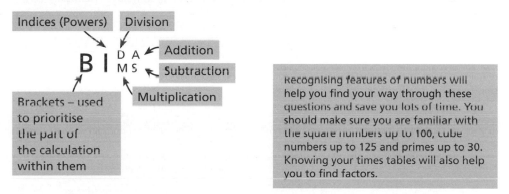

Indices (Powers)   Division

B I D A — Addition
M S — Subtraction

Brackets – used to prioritise the part of the calculation within them

Multiplication

Recognising features of numbers will help you find your way through these questions and save you lots of time. You should make sure you are familiar with the square numbers up to 100, cube numbers up to 125 and primes up to 30. Knowing your times tables will also help you to find factors.

As division is the inverse of multiplication, they are equally weighted (same with addition and subtraction). Any division can be expressed as a multiplication, e.g. $a \div 2 = a \times \frac{1}{2}$
The operation belongs to the number it is in front of.

Remember that if there is a fraction, then the top and bottom should be considered to be in brackets (re-writing this can make it clear) before doing the division. Similarly, all the calculation under a square root can be bracketed and the square root falls under 'I' (indices) in BIDMAS. A number in front of brackets means multiply, having first worked out the brackets.

Example 3.8

Showing the steps in your working, find the solutions to these.

a) $37 - 2(3 + 4 \div 2)$ *(3 marks)*

$37 - 2(3 + 4 \div 2)$

$= 37 - 2(3 + 2)$ ✓

$= 37 - 2 \times 5$ ✓

$= 37 - 10$

$= 27$ ✓

Setting out the calculations with each line below can help to keep track of what is going on. If you want to add additional working, do so at the side. The temptation can be to do something such as:

$$37 - 2(3 + 4 \div 2)$$
$$4 \div 2 = 2$$
$$2 + 3 = 5 \times 2 = 10$$
$$27$$

This is incorrect. The third line suggests $2 + 3 = 10$, which is not true. It is also somewhat confusing to follow, though it does get to the right answer in the end. If there is a fraction, writing it out in a line with brackets and a $\div$ symbol means this method can work in every case.

b) $\dfrac{37 - 2(3 + 4 \div 2)}{1 + 2^3} - 4 + \sqrt{12 \times 3}$ *(4 marks)*

$\dfrac{37 - 2(3 + 4 \div 2)}{1 + 2^3} - 4 + \sqrt{12 \times 3}$

$= 27 \div (1 + 2^3) - 4 + \sqrt{(12 \times 3)}$ ✓

$= 27 \div (1 + 8) - 4 + \sqrt{36}$ ✓

$= 27 \div 9 - 4 + 6$

$= 3 - 4 + 6$ ✓

$= -1 + 6$

$= 5$ ✓

Spotting that the calculation from part **a)** is included in part **b)** can save you time. You know the value was 27, so you can substitute it in without showing all those steps of working again (though it is good to say where it came from).

Recognising square numbers is helpful here.

3.9 Inverse Operations

Adding and subtracting are the inverse operations of each other. If you add 2 to a number, to undo that you would subtract 2. Likewise, division is the inverse of multiplication.

Example 3.9

Pallas asks Rose to think of a number. She then tells Rose to carry out the following calculations in this order:

Subtract 7, then multiply by 6, then divide by 2

a) Suggest a simplification to Pallas' instructions. *(1 mark)*

> Multiplying by 6 then dividing by 2 is the same as multiplying by 3.
> Her new instructions could be subtract 7, then multiply by 3. ✓

b) Rose says her answer is −12. Pallas says she knows what Rose's original number was. Explain how to find Rose's original number. *(2 marks)*

To find Rose's original number, do the opposite. Considering it as a function machine:

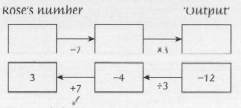

Rose's original number was 3. ✓

A common mistake is to use the inverse operations but to do them in the original order, i.e. +7 then ÷3. If you are undoing what has been done, start from the end and work backwards. A diagram can help to show this clearly.

3.10 Standard Form

Standard form is used to express very big or very small numbers. It allows you to compare and calculate with these numbers without writing, counting and dealing with long strings of zeros. You need to be able to convert from and to standard form. You also need to be able to calculate with numbers in standard form, both with and without a calculator.

Number

Example 3.10.1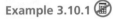

The wavelength of blue light is approximately 0.00000045 m. The wavelength of red light is approximately 7×10^{-7} m.

a) Which has the greater wavelength, and by how much? Give your answer in standard form. *(2 marks)*

The wavelength of blue light = 4.5×10^{-7} ✓

The wavelength of red light = 7×10^{-7}

$7 \times 10^{-7} - 4.5 \times 10^{-7} = 2.5 \times 10^{-7}$

Red light has the greater wavelength, by 2.5×10^{-7} m. ✓

> You can convert both numbers into standard form or into normal numbers to compare and calculate. Sometimes one way will be easier than the other. In this case, both numbers are 'of the order' $\times 10^{-7}$ so the subtraction was relatively easy, even in standard form.

Without a calculator, this can seem fairly daunting. If you can identify what makes it hard then you can find a solution.

Including a unit in your final answer is really helpful and demonstrates your understanding. It also helps you to spot where units are used and avoid mistakes in cases where units might need converting.

b) An X-ray has a wavelength that is 0.0034 times that of blue light.

What is the wavelength of this X-ray? Give your answer in standard form. *(2 marks)*

$0.0034 = 3.4 \times 10^{-3} = 34 \times 10^{-4}$

$4.5 \times 10^{-7} = 45 \times 10^{-8}$

$4.5 \times 10^{-7} \times 3.4 \times 10^{-3} = 34 \times 45 \times 10^{-4} \times 10^{-8}$

$\qquad = 1530 \times 10^{-12}$ ✓

$\qquad = 1.53 \times 10^{-9}$ m ✓

$$\begin{array}{r} 34 \\ \times\ 45 \\ \hline 170 \\ 1360 \\ \hline 1530 \end{array}$$

> By using powers of 10, you can make your calculation deal with integers and the powers of 10 separately.

> This is not yet in standard form, but candidates often lose the last mark by not realising that.

Example 3.10.2

There are estimated to be 80 000 000 000 stars in the Milky Way. A sample of four stars has a mean mass of 5.4×10^{30} kg.

If Adil assumes that this represents all the stars in the Milky Way, what would he calculate the total mass to be? *(2 marks)*

Estimate for total mass = Mean mass × Number of stars

$$= 5.4 \times 10^{30} \times 8 \times 10^{10} = 4.32 \times 10^{41} \checkmark$$

Adil would calculate the mass of all the stars in the Milky Way to be 4.32×10^{41} kg (3 s.f.) $\checkmark$

Make sure you show what you key into the calculator, as well as the answer it gives. This means you will still get method marks even if you make a mistake keying in the calculation.

3.11 Fractions and Decimals

Fractions, decimals and percentages are all different ways of expressing a number. Sometimes it makes more sense to use one form rather than another. This might make it clearer or be an easier form to work with. If multiplying two numbers, a fraction might be easier; but to understand and compare numbers, decimals could be a better option. You need to be able to convert between, and interpret, the different forms.

Example 3.11

a) Express $\frac{2}{15}$ as a decimal. *(2 marks)*

		15 times table	
$\frac{2}{15} = 2 \div 15$		15	1
$0.1\,3\,3...$		30	2
$15\overline{)2.^20^50^50...}\;\checkmark$		45	3
So $\frac{2}{15} = 0.1\dot{3}\;\checkmark$		60	4
		75	5
		90	6

Make sure you set up your written method clearly. In this case it is using short division.

Writing out the times table of the denominator (divisor) can help to save time. Don't spend too long taking it too far as you can always add more later!

If using short division, remember that you need to insert your decimal point and can continue to insert zeros after it until you have found the pattern that **recurs**. When you notice a digit repeating, you can stop doing the division as it will repeat the pattern forever. Use dots above the first and last digit in the repeating pattern (in this case, there is just one dot as only one number repeats).

b) Express 0.024 as a fully simplified fraction. *(2 marks)*

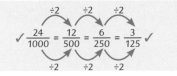

$$\checkmark\frac{24}{1000} = \frac{12}{500} = \frac{6}{250} = \frac{3}{125}\;\checkmark$$

If the decimal terminates, look at the digit furthest to the right and consider its place value. In this case the 4 is in the thousandths column, so put 24 over 1000 and then simplify.

3.12 Rounding

Often the exact value of a number, into the thousandths and beyond, doesn't really matter. Sometimes there is an obvious rounding point – for example, with money, you would always use 2 decimal places as that is the number of pence. If you measure something using a ruler, you can only be as accurate as half a millimetre, which is accurate enough for most day-to-day uses. In scientific experiments, special measuring tools provide greater accuracy.

You need to be able to round to significant figures, to decimal places and to the nearest whole number, nearest ten, nearest hundred, nearest thousand, etc. You also need to be able to consider the bounds of a rounded number.

Example 3.12

Jay works for a newspaper. Below is a page from his notebook. The newspaper has the following rules about how to write numbers in a report:

- If the number is greater than a million, then it should be reported to 2 significant figures and 'million' used as a word. For example, 5 700 000 = 5.7 million.
- All other numbers should be reported to 3 significant figures.

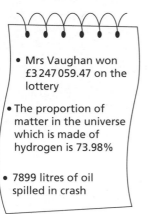

- Mrs Vaughan won £3 247 059.47 on the lottery

- The proportion of matter in the universe which is made of hydrogen is 73.98%

- 7899 litres of oil spilled in crash

a) Jay will first convert his numbers into the correct format and then write his story. What should he get for each of his numbers?

i) Mrs Vaughan's lottery win *(1 mark)*

£3.2 *million* ✓

ii) Proportion of matter in the universe that is hydrogen *(1 mark)*

74.0% ✓	If the final digit, when rounded, is 0 you should still leave it in, even after the decimal point. This shows that there are 3 s.f. since the zero is still a significant figure.

iii) Amount of oil spilled in crash *(1 mark)*

7900 *l* ✓

In an earlier story, Jay said that "4780 people had been evacuated after flooding hit 1400 homes across the north of England".

b) Write the **error interval** for both of the numbers quoted above. *(2 marks)*

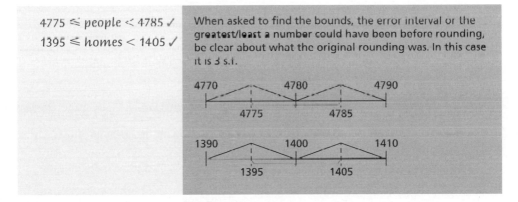

$4775 \leqslant$ people < 4785 ✓
$1395 \leqslant$ homes < 1405 ✓

When asked to find the bounds, the error interval or the greatest/least a number could have been before rounding, be clear about what the original rounding was. In this case it is 3 s.f.

3.13 Rounding and Estimation

If you are asked to estimate, you are expected to round each number to 1 significant figure and carry out the calculation with these less accurate, but easier to work with, values.

Example 3.13

Karl is at the supermarket and has £20. He doesn't want to spend more than £20, so he uses estimation to help keep track of how much he has spent as he goes around the store. These are the items in his basket so far:

a) Karl wants to buy a book that costs £2.89. By rounding the prices to 1 significant figure, estimate how much he has spent so far and decide if he should put the book in his basket or not. *(2 marks)*

Estimation – round to 1 s.f.	
Carrots:	0.60
Bread: 3 × 0.90 =	2.70
Milk:	1.00
Pasta: 4 × 2.00 =	8.00
Pasta sauce:	3.00
Tomatoes: 2 × 1.00 =	2.00 ✓
	17.30
20 − 17.30 = 2.70	2.70 < 2.89

When estimating, you only round the initial numbers to 1 s.f. Every time you round a number, some error creeps in. If you repeatedly round a value, the error can become huge in comparison to the starting number.
If you are 16 years old, you are 20 to the nearest 10, which is 30 to the nearest 30. That is 50 to the nearest 50 and that would be 100 to the nearest 100. If you were told at 16 that your age is 100 to the nearest 100, it clearly isn't accurate.

Based on the estimate of his costs so far,
Karl doesn't have enough money to buy the book as well. ✓

b) Jaz is also shopping and has a voucher that gives her £2.50 off if she spends more than £30. Jaz says that if she rounds up each price to the nearest pound, she can be sure that she will get the money off.
Is Jaz right? Explain your answer. *(1 mark)*

Jaz is not correct. By rounding up each answer, she will think she has spent more than she actually has. Jaz should round down each price to be sure. ✓

3.14 Limits of Accuracy – Error Intervals

Truncation and rounding can be used to simplify an answer. You use them all the time. For example, if you are asked your age, you may truncate it to the nearest year. Sometimes the inherent inaccuracy of measurement means that a value is rounded. For example, if you draw a 14 mm long line using a standard ruler, it is likely to be 14 mm to the nearest half millimetre. More accurate instruments can reduce the error but even then the measurement won't be completely accurate. If a number is truncated or rounded, it can be important to know what the greatest and least value could be.

Example 3.14

Suz is cycling in a velodrome. She is training for a long distance ride, so she does 100 laps at a constant speed. It takes Suz 25 seconds, to the nearest second, to complete each lap.

a) What is the error interval for Suz's lap time? *(2 marks)*

25 seconds to nearest second
$1 \div 2$, split 0.5 seconds
$24.5 \leqslant t < 25.5$ ✓ ✓

Suz's coach says that she might not have time to complete 100 laps as she only has 40 minutes left. Her coach has truncated this to 2 significant figures.

b) What is the error interval for the time that Suz has left (T)? *(2 marks)*

$40 \leqslant T < 41$ ✓ ✓

As the number has been truncated, the stated value forms the **lower bound** (bottom of the error interval). The number could be 40.99999999 but truncate to 40 (truncated to 2 s.f.).

c) What is the error interval for the number of full laps that Suz will complete in her remaining time? *(4 marks)*

Most: Use her lowest lap time and the longest time on track.
$41 \times 60 = 2460$ seconds
$2460 \div 24.5 = 100.4081633\ldots$ ✓

Least: Use her highest lap time and the lowest time on track.
$40 \times 60 = 2400$ seconds
$2400 \div 25.5 = 94.11764706\ldots$ ✓
$94 \leqslant \text{laps} \leqslant 100$ ✓ ✓

As the question asks for the number of complete laps, you need to round down both your **upper bound** and your lower bound. Both these values are possible so both have the 'less than or equal to' inequality symbol.

3.15 Roots and Indices

Roots and indices are inverse operations (this is why roots fall under 'I' in BIDMAS). Indices, also known as powers, are an operation that multiplies a number by itself a number of times. For example, 4^3 (said 'four to the power 3' or 'four cubed') means $4 \times 4 \times 4 = 64$. Roots do the opposite. The cube root of 64, $\sqrt[3]{64} = 4$.

Example 3.15

a) Evaluate 4^0. *(1 mark)*

$4^0 = 1$ ✓   'Evaluate' means you need to find the final numerical answer.

b) Simplify $\dfrac{3^5 \times 3^{-2}}{3^4}$ *(3 marks)*   'Simplify', in this context, means that you combine the indices where possible.

$\dfrac{3^5 \times 3^{-2}}{3^4} = \dfrac{3^{(5 + -2)}}{3^4} ✓ = \dfrac{3^3}{3^4}$

$= 3^{(3-4)} ✓ = 3^{-1} ✓$

If you know there is a rule for multiplying indices with the same base but cannot remember what it is, think of a simple example. For example, $2^3 \times 2^2 = 2 \times 2 \times 2 \times 2 \times 2 = 2^5$. From this you can see that adding the powers works.

c) Evaluate $\dfrac{3^3 + \sqrt{25}}{2^5}$ *(3 marks)*

$\dfrac{3^3 + \sqrt{25}}{2^5} = \dfrac{27 + 5}{32}$ ✓ ✓

$= \dfrac{32}{32}$

$= 1$ ✓

$3^3 = 3 \times 3 \times 3$
$= 9 \times 3$
$= 27$

$2^5 = 2 \times 2 \times 2 \times 2 \times 2$
$= 4 \times 2 \times 2 \times 2$
$= 8 \times 2 \times 2$
$= 16 \times 2$
$= 32$

You are expected to be able to recognise powers of 2, 3, 4, and 5. You can use your knowledge and understanding of what powers/indices are to help calculate anything that you don't know, or to check.

3.16 Exact Solutions Involving Irrational Numbers

When a number is expressed accurately, there can be no rounding or truncation. Some numbers can be written exactly in decimal form. Others can have recurring decimals and these can be written as a fraction. If a number can be written as a fraction, it is **rational**.

Irrational numbers cannot be written as a fraction as they have a never-ending chain of decimals that have no repeating pattern. These numbers are expressed 'exactly' by using a symbol. The example that you come across in GCSE is the number π. You can put it into your calculator to get a decimal but it will always be a rounded version as the decimals go on forever. If a question asks for an exact answer, you should leave your answer with π in it. Lots of calculators give an exact value as an answer – try yours and see by typing in $3 \times \pi$. Keep an eye out for the key word 'exact'.

Example 3.16

a) The diameter of a circle is 18 cm.
   Find the exact area of the circle. *(2 marks)*

> Area of a circle $A = \pi r^2$
> $= \pi 9^2$ ✓
> $= 81\pi \, cm^2$ ✓

b) The circumference of a circle is 15 cm.
   What is the exact length of the diameter? *(2 marks)*

> Circumference of a circle $C = \pi d$
> $15 = \pi d$ ✓
> $d = \frac{15}{\pi}$ cm ✓

> If there is a division in your calculation, leaving it in fraction form can be easiest. The π symbol can appear in the denominator of a fraction.

3.17 Checking Answers Using Approximation

When doing any calculations, it is useful to be able to check your answer. By using estimation and common sense, you can often spot mistakes in calculations. There are lots of small things that can show if the answer is correct or not. The more time you spend working with numbers, the more familiar these will become   and the fewer mistakes you are likely to make.

Example 3.17

Check the answers to the questions below. Use a method of your choice to determine if the answer is definitely incorrect or probably correct.

a) $476 \times 572 = 20273$ *(1 mark)*

> This is incorrect because:
>
> - An even number multiplied by an even number should give an even answer. The answer given, 20 273, is odd.
> - Estimating the answer $\approx 500 \times 600 \approx 300000$. 20 273 is not approximately 300 000.
> - An under-estimate of the answer would be $400 \times 500 = 200000$. $200000 > 20273$ so the answer 20 273 is incorrect. ✓

> Any one of these reasons is enough. A few are listed in each case to give examples. The reasoning must be complete. It is easy to think it is enough to say that an estimate would be 300 000, but you need to explain why this value shows that 20 273 cannot be right.

b) $52 + \sqrt{481 - 103} = 71.4$ (3 s.f.) *(2 marks)*

> Estimation $52 + \sqrt{481 - 103} \approx 50 + \sqrt{500 - 100}$ ✓
>
> $\approx 50 + \sqrt{400}$
>
> $\approx 50 + 20$
>
> ≈ 70
>
> As $70 \approx 71.4$, this supports that the answer is probably correct. ✓

Make sure your answer is complete with explanation and conclusion.

c) The length of a man's femur (leg bone) is 26.74% of his height. A femur has a length of 45 cm. So the height of the man is 425 cm. *(1 mark)*

> The answer is incorrect because:
>
> * 425 cm = 4.25 m
>   A door is 2 m tall, which is equivalent to a tall human. This height is more than double that, so it is unrealistic. ✓
>
> * The height is approximately four times the length of the femur (as 26.74% ≈ 25%), which would be 180 cm. This is considerably less than the given answer.

Estimation might not catch small errors but it will help to detect big ones. If a question is in context, consider if it makes sense as an answer.

3.18 Contextual Number Problems

Number skills can be tested through a contextual problem – it can feel a bit like reading a story. Your skills lie in spotting the mathematical elements in the question and translating these into a series of calculations.

Example 3.18

Karen works for a factory that makes cake decorations. One of the products is chocolate star sprinkles. Every kilogram of chocolate makes one thousand stars. The factory sells the stars in packets of 120. Each kilogram of chocolate costs £2.50. The packaging for each packet costs 20p. The packets of stars are sold for £1.50 each. In a day the factory uses 225 kg of chocolate.

Assuming all packets produced are sold, how much profit will the factory make in one day? *(6 marks)*

Highlighting key information can help you get the details from the question.

Number of stars made in one day = Amount of chocolate × 1000

$$= 225 × 1000$$

$$= \underline{225\,000 \text{ stars a day}} ✓$$

Cost of chocolate = Amount of chocolate × Cost of chocolate = 225 × 2.50

$$= 225 × 2 + 225 × \frac{1}{2} = 450 + 112.5$$

$$= \underline{£562.50 \text{ (cost of chocolate)}} ✓$$

Packets made each day = Number of stars ÷ Number of stars in a packet

$$= 225\,000 ÷ 120 = 22\,500 ÷ 12$$

$$= \underline{1875 \text{ packets made each day}} ✓$$

12	1
24	2
36	3
48	4
60	5
72	6
84	7
96	8
108	9
120	10

$$12\overline{)22\,500}$$ → 0 1 8 7 5

Sale price of packets of stars = Number of packets × Price

$$= 1875 × 1.50 = 1875 + 1875 × \frac{1}{2} = 1875 + 937.5$$

$$= \underline{£2812.50 \text{ income per day}} ✓$$

Cost of packaging = Number of packets × Cost

$$= 1875 × 0.2 = 1875 × 2 ÷ 10$$

$$= 3750 ÷ 10$$

$$= \underline{£375.00 \text{ (cost of packaging)}} ✓$$

Profit = Income − Outgoings (cost of chocolate and packaging)

$$= 2812.50 − 562.50 − 375.00$$

$$= \underline{£1875.00} ✓$$

```
  2812.50
−  562.50
  2250.00
```

```
  2250.00
−  375.00
  1875.00
```

Plan the steps to your answer. There is no correct order. By explaining what each calculation does, you will be able to use the information you find more easily. The answer below has all the same steps and the same final answer but is much harder to understand. It also uses the '=' symbol incorrectly.

$$225 × 1000 = 225\,000 ÷ 120 = 1875$$
$$225 × 2.5 = 562.5 + 20p × 1875$$
$$= 937.5$$
$$1875 × 1.5 = 2812.5 − 937.5$$
$$= \underline{1875}$$

 For more on the topics covered in this chapter, see pages 8–13, 26–31, 56–57 & 102–103 of the Collins Edexcel Maths Foundation Revision Guide.

Number: Key Notes

- Integers are whole numbers including zero and negatives. Multiples and factors are part of 'whole number theory' so you will be working with integers.
- When comparing numbers in different forms, you need to be able to convert between fractions (F), decimals (D) and percentages (P).

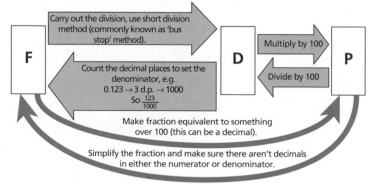

- There are some **sets** of numbers with special properties which can help you to answer questions. It is useful to be able to recognise the numbers as part of these sets:
  - **prime numbers**: 2, 3, 5, 7, 11, 13, 17, 19, 23, 29,...
  - **square numbers**: 1, 4, 9, 16, 25, 36, 49, 64, 81, 100, ...
  - **cube numbers**: 1, 8, 27, 64, ..., 1000, ...
- It is also useful to recognise and learn the equivalent decimals to key fractions, for example: $\frac{1}{2}$ = 0.5, $\frac{1}{4}$ = 0.25, $\frac{3}{4}$ = 0.75, $\frac{1}{3}$ = 0.3333 ...
- You can always find the decimal equivalent by dividing the numbers in a fraction, but if a question refers to $0.5x$, it can be useful to think of this as 'half of x'.
- Indices and roots are important and you need to be able to evaluate and simplify numbers. 'Evaluate' means find the value without the **index**. 'Simplify' means to leave in index form but written as simply as possible.
- Standard form is used to express very large and very small numbers. The form is a single non-zero digit in front of the decimal point, then $\times 10^a$. For example, you can write 0.00000000103 as 1.03×10^{-9}.
- If the question asks for an accurate answer, you should leave your answer as 3π, for example, rather than as 9.4247779... This is because however many of the decimals you write out, the number cannot be written completely accurately as a decimal.
- A number that has been rounded or truncated is inaccurate; this is why you save rounding until the end of a question. You need to be able to find the error interval of numbers that have been rounded. Watch out for the difference between rounding and truncating. If a number is truncated, it is literally just cut off. So 9.4 truncated to 2 s.f. would have an error interval of $9.4 \leqslant x < 9.5$. But 9.4 rounded to 2 s.f. would have an error interval of $9.35 \leqslant x < 9.45$.
- With worded problems, the skill being tested is your understanding of what operations are needed to find the solution. Highlight or underline key information from the question and show as much working as you can.

4   Algebra

Mathematics has its own language and conventions to ensure that anyone can understand what is happening. Algebra helps mathematicians to simplify problems in the real world so that they can be considered objectively and more easily solved. At times this can seem a bit confusing but usually it is done so that the meaning can be conveyed with as little writing as possible.

4.1 Manipulating Algebraic Expressions

Being able to confidently manipulate algebraic **expressions** is fundamental to success in algebra. It allows you to use different forms to look for different information.

Expanding and Simplifying Algebraic Expressions

Algebraic expressions can be simplified by collecting like **terms**. Questions may ask you to expand brackets and then simplify.

Example 4.1.1

Which of the following are equivalent to $4a - 3b + 4$?
Show working to justify your answer. *(3 marks)*

$$2a - b + a + 2b + 4 + a \qquad\qquad 2(2a - 4) + 3(4 - b) \qquad\qquad 6(2a - \tfrac{1}{2}b) - 4(2a + 1)$$

As the question says you must justify your answer, your method needs to be clear. For each expression you should simplify to check whether it is equal. Don't forget to state for each one whether or not it is equal.

$2a - b + a + 2b + 4 + a$	$2(2a - 4) + 3(4 - b)$	$6(2a - \tfrac{1}{2}b) - 4(2a + 1)$
$2a + a + a - b + 2b + 4$	$4a - 8 + 12 - 3b$	$12a - 3b - 8a - 4$
$4a + b + 4$	$4a - 3b - 8 + 12$	$12a - 8a - 3b - 4$
Not equal ✓	$4a - 3b + 4$	$4a - 3b - 4$
	Equal ✓	Not equal ✓

It is a good idea to rewrite the expression with the like terms next to each other before you start combining them.

Make sure you keep the sign with the number.

When multiplying out the brackets, you might find it helpful to use a grid, in which case draw it at the side.

	$2a$	-4
2	$4a$	-8

	4	$-b$
3	12	$-3b$

On this one, you need to be careful with the negative as it means you are multiplying both terms by -4.

	$2a$	$-\tfrac{1}{2}b$
6	$12a$	$-3b$

	$2a$	$+1$
-4	$-8a$	-4

Expanding Binomials

Binomials are expressions with two terms ('bi' means 'two' and 'nomials' refers to the terms). At foundation tier, you will only be expected to expand double brackets but this can involve fractions or **surds**. There are different methods for multiplying out brackets and it can be tempting to do them in your head, but showing a clear method is the best way to make sure you get full marks.

Example 4.1.2

Express $(x + \sqrt{5})(x - \sqrt{5})$ in the form $ax^2 + bx + c$. *(2 marks)*

Two of the most common methods for multiplying out brackets are shown. If you use another method, e.g. FOIL, make sure you show your working clearly.

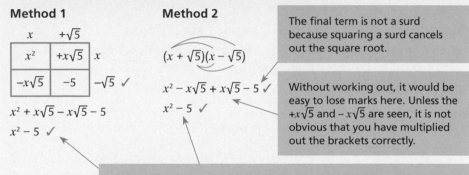

Method 1

	x	$+\sqrt{5}$
x	x^2	$+x\sqrt{5}$
$-\sqrt{5}$ ✓	$-x\sqrt{5}$	-5

$x^2 + x\sqrt{5} - x\sqrt{5} - 5$

$x^2 - 5$ ✓

Method 2

$(x + \sqrt{5})(x - \sqrt{5})$

$x^2 - x\sqrt{5} + x\sqrt{5} - 5$ ✓

$x^2 - 5$ ✓

The final term is not a surd because squaring a surd cancels out the square root.

Without working out, it would be easy to lose marks here. Unless the $+x\sqrt{5}$ and $-x\sqrt{5}$ are seen, it is not obvious that you have multiplied out the brackets correctly.

The answer is now in the form $ax^2 + bx + c$, where $a = 1$, $b = 0$ and $c = -5$.

Factorising

Factorising is the process of putting the brackets back into an expression.

Example 4.1.3 (single brackets)

Fully factorise the expression $18a^2 - 6a$. *(1 mark)*

You are looking for numbers and letters that are factors of both terms. Fully factorising means you are taking out the highest common factor from both terms, meaning in this case just $6(3a^2 - a)$ would not be fully factorised and therefore not get the mark.

$6a(3a - 1)$ ✓

	$3a$	-1
$6a$	$18a^2$	$-6a$

To find the terms left inside the brackets, divide each one by $6a$. The -1 at the end is easily forgotten but remember that anything divided by itself will be 1.

Multiplying out checks that your factorisation is correct.

Example 4.1.4 (double brackets)

Fully factorise $x^2 + 2x - 8$. *(2 marks)*

First make sure your **quadratic** is in the form $x^2 + bx + c$.
Look for two numbers that multiply to give c and add together to give b. Writing out the factors of c can help if you cannot see it straight away. The two numbers will go into double brackets, giving you the final answer.

$x^2 + 2x - 8$

Product of −8	Sum of +2
−1 × 8	no
2 × −4	no
−2 × 4	yes

Some students will use a different method to factorise. If you use a different method, that is fine.
Whatever method you use, multiplying out to check your answers ensures you have factorised correctly.

$(x - 2)(x + 4)$ ✓

	x	2	
	x^2	$-2x$	x
	$+4x$	-8	$+4$

There is no mark for this step but it is the most important as this is how you know you have got it right.

$x^2 - 2x + 4x - 8$

$= x^2 + 2x - 8$

Indices

Questions involving indices can be either numerical or algebraic, but the same rules apply in both situations. If you ever forget the rules, you can always write them out and simplify as normal, for example $a^3 \times a^2 = (a \times a \times a) \times (a \times a) = a^5$. It is always better to be sure about things than try to do them quickly. If you are unsure, but worried about time, put the answer you think and draw a star next to the question so you know to come back to it if you have time.

Example 4.1.5

The area of a rectangle is $(3a^3b)^2$ and one of the side lengths is $3ab^2$.

Find the other side length, giving your answer in its simplest form.

Area = $(3a^3b)^2$ $3ab^2$

(3 marks)

Algebra

Start the question by thinking about what you know and what you need to know. You have been given the area and one of the sides. The formula to find the area of a rectangle can be rearranged to find the other side.

unknown

Area = (Length) × Width

$\frac{Area}{Width}$ = Length

$\frac{(3a^3b)^2}{3ab^2}$ ✓

$\frac{9a^6b^2}{3ab^2}$

$3a^5$ ✓✓

Substituting the given information into this formula gives an expression to simplify.

This means $(3a^3b) \times (3a^3b)$. You can either write it out or remember the rule that brackets mean the powers are multiplied.

4.2 Formulae

A formula is an equation that enables you to convert, or find a value, using other known values. There are some formulae you will need to know and these can be found in Chapter 10. Other formulae will be given as part of the question if needed.

Example 4.2

A ball is dropped from a height of 12 m. Its initial velocity is 0 m/s and it travels with a constant acceleration of 10 m/s².

Find the time it takes to reach the ground. Give your answer to 1 decimal place.

You may use the following formula:

$s = ut + \frac{1}{2}at^2$ where a is constant acceleration, u is initial velocity, v is final velocity, s is displacement from the position when $t = 0$ and t is time taken. *(3 marks)*

You should have seen the SUVAT equations before and be comfortable using them. If you aren't familiar with them, see Chapter 10, but they will be given in the question if needed.

$s = 12$ $12 = (0)t + \frac{1}{2}(10)t^2$ ✓

$u = 0$ $12 = 5t^2$

$v = ✗$ $t^2 = \frac{12}{5}$ ✓

$a = 10$ $t = \sqrt{\frac{12}{5}}$

$t = ?$ $t = 1.549$

     $t = 1.5$ seconds ✓

It is always a good idea to write out which bits of information you have and which you are looking for before you start.

4.3 Functions

A **function** is like a machine where there are inputs and outputs. The function tells you the relationship between the inputs and outputs.

Example 4.3

The functions f, g and h are such that $f(x) = \frac{x-9}{2}$ and $g(x) = x^2 + 9$.

a) Find the value of f(5). *(1 mark)*

$f(x) = \frac{5-9}{2}$

Substitute $x = 5$ into the function.

$= \frac{-4}{2}$

$= -2 \checkmark$

b) Find the value of g(a + 1). *(2 marks)*

$g(a + 1) - (a + 1)^2 + 9$

Having a letter makes it seem more complicated but you are doing the same thing here. Substitute $x = a + 1$ into the function.

	u	$+1$
a	a^2	$+a$
$+1$	$+a$	$+1$

$u^2 + u + u + 1$

$= a^2 + 2a + 1 \checkmark$

Use your normal method to multiply out double brackets, making your method clear.

$a^2 + 2a + 1 + 9$

$= a^2 + 2a + 10 \checkmark$

4.4 Equations and Inequalities

To be able to use algebra to understand the real world, you will need to be confident setting up equations from information. This will often draw upon other areas of mathematics, in particular geometry and measures. In the rest of this chapter, many of the examples will be put into contexts. It is important to think about the implications of the context to check whether your answer seems sensible. The questions might not always be completely realistic, but if you get a negative age, time or length you know that there is a mistake to check.

Linear Equations

Sometimes students guess values to find the answers to linear equations but you will need to make sure you have a good method to be able to deal with harder equations and ensure you get full marks. Teachers will explain this topic in different ways. The sides of the equation need to be kept balanced so that whatever is done to one side is also done to the other. If you have a different method, make sure you still show working out. You can always check your final answer by substituting it into the original equation to check it gives you the correct solution.

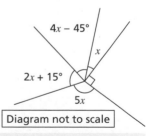

$4x - 45°$

x

$2x + 15°$

$5x$

Diagram not to scale

Example 4.4.1

Find the value of x in the diagram. *(3 marks)*

Notice that the diagram is not drawn to scale, so don't be tempted to use your protractor to measure the angles.

$5x + 90 + x + 2x + 15 + 4x - 45 = 360°$ ✓

$5x + x + 2x + 4x + 90 + 15 - 45 = 360°$

$12x + 60 = 360$

$\quad -60 \quad -60$

$\dfrac{12x}{12} = \dfrac{300}{12}$

$\quad x = 25°$ ✓ ✓

You need to use some of your angle knowledge here to realise that angles at a point add up to 360° and that there is a right angle which is 90°. To set up the equation, put all the angles on the left-hand side and then this is equal to 360°.

The equation can now be solved normally to find the value of x.

Example 4.4.2

Triangle ABC is an equilateral triangle. The lengths are measured in cm.

Find the perimeter of the triangle. *(4 marks)*

Because the triangle is equilateral, all three sides must be the same length. This can be used to find the value of x. Any two sides can be put equal to each other to form an equation.

$8x - 4 = 2x + 5$

$-2x \quad\quad -2x$ ✓

$6x - 4 = 5$

$+4 \quad +4$

$\dfrac{6x}{6} = \dfrac{9}{6}$

$x = \dfrac{3}{2}$ ✓

There are x values on both sides of the equation so the first thing to do is remove them from the right-hand side.

$P = 8x - 4 + 4x + 2 + 2x + 5$

$P = 14x + 3$ ✓

$P = 14 \times \dfrac{3}{2} + 3$

$P = \dfrac{\overset{7}{\cancel{14}} \times 3}{\cancel{2}} + 3$

$P = 21 + 3$

$P = 24$ cm ✓

Answers to equations aren't always integers and it is usually best to leave them as fractions. You haven't finished yet! The question is looking for the perimeter.

Find the perimeter in terms of x and then substitute in the value you have just found.

Inequalities

Inequalities are solved in the same way as linear equations, the only difference being that if you multiply or divide by a negative, the direction of the inequality sign should be reversed.

Example 4.4.3

a) Suzie represents the inequality $-\dfrac{5}{2} < x \leqslant 3$ on the number line. Is she correct? *(2 marks)*

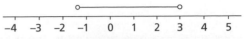

Suzie is not correct. A filled in circle should be used to represent less than or equal to and she has used an empty circle for both. ✓

The circle for $-\dfrac{5}{2}$ is drawn at $-\dfrac{3}{2}$ so is in the wrong place. ✓

If a question asks whether someone is correct, you are looking for any mistakes they might have made. In this case there are two mistakes.

b) What is the smallest integer that would satisfy the inequality $-\frac{5}{2} < x \leqslant 3$? *(1 mark)*

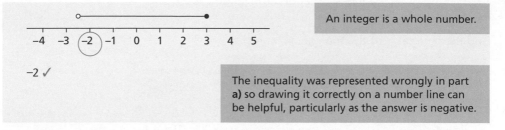

An integer is a whole number.

-2 ✓

The inequality was represented wrongly in part **a)** so drawing it correctly on a number line can be helpful, particularly as the answer is negative.

Example 4.4.4

Anna is making a run for her chickens. She has decided that the run should be rectangular with one side 1 m longer than the other. She has a maximum of 22 m of fencing.

Find algebraically the possible length of the shortest side of the run. *(3 marks)*

If you haven't been given a diagram, a good place to start is with a sketch.

As one side is 1 m longer than the other, the first side can be x and the second $x + 1$.

$$x + x + 1 + x + x + 1 \leqslant 22 \checkmark$$
$$4x + 2 \leqslant 22$$
$$-2 \quad -2 \checkmark$$
$$\frac{4x}{4} \leqslant \frac{20}{4}$$
$$x \leqslant 5\,\text{m} \checkmark$$

The fencing is around the outside of the run, so it forms the perimeter of the rectangle.

Linear Simultaneous Equations

Example 4.4.5

Boris and Amina have made cakes and biscuits to sell on a stall at the school fair to raise money. Amina sells her cakes for 30p each and her biscuits for 50p each. Boris charges 70p per cake and 50p per biscuit.

Amina makes £8 and Boris makes £10. They both sell the same number of cakes and the same number of biscuits.

How many biscuits and cakes did they each sell? *(5 marks)*

Let c be the number of cakes sold.

Let b be the number of biscuits sold.

Amina	Boris
$30c + 50b = 800$	$70c + 50b = 1000$
$3c + 5b = 80$ ✓	$7c + 5b = 100$ ✓

$B - A \quad 7c + 5b = 100$

$(-) \quad 3c + 5b = 80$ ✓

$\dfrac{4c}{4} = \dfrac{20}{4}$

$\qquad c = 5$ ✓

Substitute into A $\quad 3(5) + 5b = 80$

$\qquad\qquad\qquad\qquad 15 + 5b = 80$

$\qquad\qquad\qquad\qquad\qquad 5b = 65$

$\qquad\qquad\qquad\qquad\qquad b = 13$ ✓

Check in B $\quad 7(5) + 5(13)$

$\qquad\qquad\qquad = 35 + 65$

$\qquad\qquad\qquad = 100$

$\qquad\qquad\qquad\quad\begin{array}{r} 13 \\ \times\ 5 \\ \hline 6\,5 \\ \hline \end{array}$

The first thing to do with this question is set up your equations. Begin by defining the **variables**. You could use any letters you like but it makes sense to use ones that fit with the context.

When setting up the equations, you need to check the units – the price of the cakes and biscuits is given in pence and the amount made is given in pounds. Both have been expressed in pence in the working. This makes the numbers quite big. Both equations can be simplified by dividing through by 10.

Because the **coefficient** of b is 5 in both equations, you can use elimination straight away. If you prefer to use **substitution**, that is fine – you will get the same answer.

Where you have a calculation like 13×5, it is a good idea to do it at the side of the page so that the examiner can see your method but it doesn't interrupt the flow of the algebra. There aren't marks for the final check but it tells you that you've got it right and that is important for your peace of mind.

Solving Quadratics

To solve quadratics, first you need to factorise as shown earlier (see page 32). Each bracket can then be put equal to 0, leaving you with two simple linear equations to solve.

Example 4.4.6

The hypotenuse of a right-angled triangle is 13 cm and the length of the second longest side is 7 cm longer than the length of the shortest side.

Find the length of the shortest side. *(4 marks)*

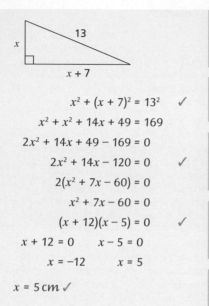

$x^2 + (x + 7)^2 = 13^2$ ✓

$x^2 + x^2 + 14x + 49 = 169$

$2x^2 + 14x + 49 - 169 = 0$

$2x^2 + 14x - 120 = 0$ ✓

$2(x^2 + 7x - 60) = 0$

$x^2 + 7x - 60 = 0$

$(x + 12)(x - 5) = 0$ ✓

$x + 12 = 0$ $x - 5 = 0$

$x = -12$ $x = 5$

$x = 5\,cm$ ✓

The question is talking about a triangle so a good starting point is to draw one and put on everything you know.

You have been given two sides of a right-angled triangle so can use **Pythagoras' theorem**.

Taking out a factor of 2 makes the quadratic easier to factorise. Dividing both sides by 2 leaves a much simpler quadratic.

Because the value of c is negative, you are looking for one positive and one negative factor with a difference of 7.

Only one of the answers is sensible here so 5 cm is the answer.

4.5 Graphs

Drawing and using graphs to model the real world is used in many different areas of life, from businesses which want to maximise profits to engineers who want to know the path an object will take when propelled.

Coordinates

When describing a point on a graph, a pair of coordinates is used. You can be asked to find the **midpoint** of two points. This can be found by adding together each of the coordinates and halving them, which can be written as $\left(\frac{x_1 + x_2}{2}, \frac{y_1 + y_2}{2}\right)$.

Example 4.5.1

The diagram shows a square. Point D has the coordinates (–7, –5) and point E has the coordinates (1, –5).

Find the coordinates of point C, which is the midpoint of points A and E. *(3 marks)*

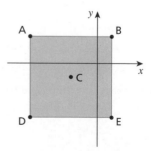

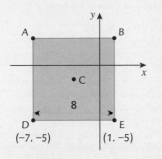

When given a diagram, it is a good idea to draw on all of the information that you have been given or can easily work out. To work out the coordinates of the midpoint, you need to know the coordinates of points A and E. E is given in the question but A is not. Because it is a square, you know that the side lengths are the same.

$-5 + 8 = 3$

Point A $(-7, 3)$ ✓

The length of side DE is 8, which means that the y-coordinate of A must be 8 higher than -5. The x-coordinate is in line with D so will be the same.

x-coordinate of C

$\frac{-7 + 1}{2} = \frac{-6}{2} = -3$ ✓

y-coordinate of C

$\frac{3 + 5}{2} = \frac{-2}{2} = -1$

The coordinates of the midpoint can now be found.

Point C $(-3, -1)$ ✓

Plotting and Using Graphs

Example 4.5.2

a) Complete the table of values for $y = x^2 - x - 2$. *(2 marks)*

x	−2	−1	0	1	2	3
y			−2		0	4

x	−2	−1	0	1	2	3
y	4	0	−2	−2	0	4	✓✓

Do your working out below or at the side of the table.

$(-2)^2 - (-2) - 2 = 4 + 2 - 2 = 4$

$(-1)^2 - (-1) - 2 = 1 + 1 - 2 = 0$

$(1)^2 - 1 - 2 = -2$

If you use a calculator, make sure to put in the brackets when squaring a negative.

b) On the same axes, plot the graphs of $y = x^2 - x - 2$ and $y = \frac{1}{2}x + 2$ between $x = -2$ and $x = 4$. *(3 marks)*

x	-2	0	2	4
y	1	2	3	4

$\frac{1}{2} \times -2 + 2 = -1 + 2 = 1$

$\frac{1}{2} \times 0 + 2 = 0 + 2 = 2$

$\frac{1}{2} \times 2 + 2 = 1 + 2 = 3$

$\frac{1}{2} \times 4 + 2 = 2 + 2 = 4$

You already have a table of coordinates for the quadratic and should draw a similar table for the line graph. Go for four points so that if you make a mistake it will show as a point that does not lie on your straight line. Because the first thing you need to do is halve the x-coordinate, it is good to choose even numbers.

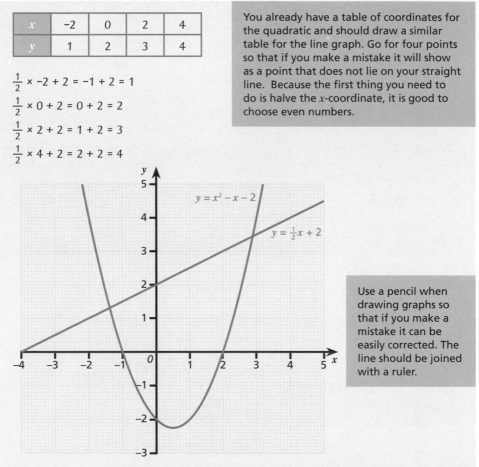

Use a pencil when drawing graphs so that if you make a mistake it can be easily corrected. The line should be joined with a ruler.

✓✓ for line

✓ for quadratic

A quadratic is a smooth curve so don't use a ruler this time. In between the points $(0, -2)$ and $(1, -2)$ the curve continues to go down a little further before turning and coming back up. If you draw a straight line here, you will lose a mark.

Your graphs should always go all the way to the edges of the grid.

c) Find the approximate solutions to $x^2 - x - 2 = \frac{1}{2}x + 2$. *(2 marks)*

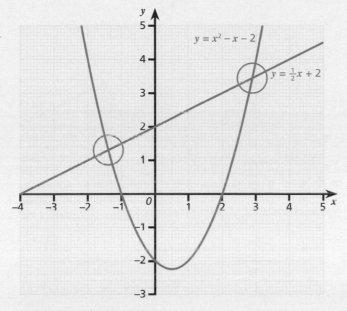

$x = -1.4$ ✓ and $x = 2.9$ ✓

> Solutions to **simultaneous equations** like this can be found by looking for the **intersections** of the two graphs. In this case there will be two answers. Try to be as accurate as you can but there will be a range of values allowed to take into account differences in candidates' graphs.

Equations of Straight Lines

The general equation of a straight line is $y = mx + c$, where m is the **gradient** and c is the y-**intercept**.

Algebra

Example 4.5.3 (identifying line graphs)

The graph shows three lines.

Match the three lines to the equations, giving reasons for your answers. *(3 marks)*

1   $y = 2x - 1$

2   $y = -\frac{1}{3}x + 4$

3   $y = 2x + 2$

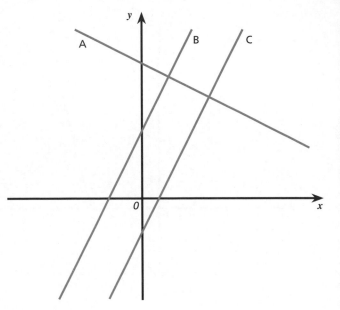

Line A has a negative gradient so it must be equation 2. ✓

Lines B and C are parallel so must be equations 1 and 3.

Line C has a negative y-intercept so is equation 1. ✓

Line B has a positive gradient and a positive y-intercept so is equation 3. ✓

Simply matching up the lines and equations wouldn't score you any marks – the explanations are needed.

Example 4.5.4 (using line graphs)

A line passes through the points A (0, 4) and B (4, 2) as shown in the diagram. The line passing through the points B and D has a gradient of 2.

Find the area of the triangle BCD. *(5 marks)*

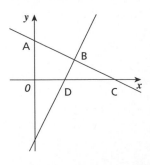

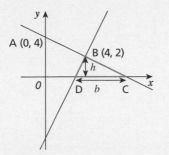

Adding everything you know on to the diagram can be very helpful with this sort of question. Drawing in the triangle can help you to see the pieces of information you already have and to identify what you need to work out.

To find the area of the triangle, you need to know the base and the height. The height is the y-coordinate of point B so is given in the question. To find the base, you need to know the x-intercepts of both lines. These can be found from the equations of the lines.

Gradient of AB

$$m = \frac{2-4}{4-0} = \frac{2}{4} = \frac{-1}{2}$$

Line AB $y = \frac{-1}{2}x + 4$ ✓

When there are a lot of steps and more than one line, it can be easy to get confused so label any working out with which line you are working on.

$$0 = \frac{-1}{2}x + 4$$

$$\frac{1}{2}x = 4$$

$$x = 8 \quad ✓$$

C is (8, 0).

For line AB you already know the y-intercept, so you can write down the equation of the line.

Point C is the x-intercept of line AB and the y-coordinate is 0, so this can be substituted in to find the x-coordinate.

Gradient of BD

$$m = 2$$

Line BD $2 = 2(4) + c$ ✓

$$2 = 8 + c$$

$$c = 2 - 8$$

$$c = -6$$

So $y = 2x - 6$

At $y = 0$ $0 = 2x - 6$

$$2x = 6$$

$$x = 3 \quad ✓$$

D is (3, 0).

You are told that the gradient of the second line is 2 and you know it goes through the point (4, 2), so you can use this to find the equation.

The base of the triangle is $8 - 3 = 5$

$$A = \frac{1}{2} \times b \times h$$

$$A = \frac{1}{2} \times 5 \times 2$$

$$A = 5 \ units^2 \quad ✓$$

With all of the information, you can now use the normal formula for the area of a triangle.

Real-life Graphs

Graphs can be used to show real-life situations and give a picture of what has happened. They are like a visual story of what has happened.

Example 4.5.5

The distance–time graph shows Klaudia's morning run. She runs to her friend's house, stays for a little while and then returns home.

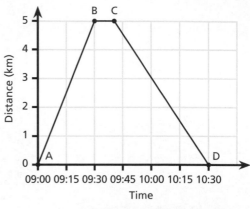

a) Calculate the gradient from point A to point B. *(2 marks)*

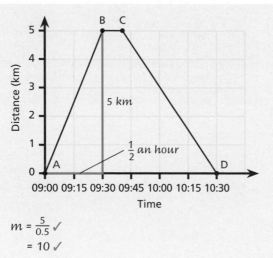

Gradient is $\frac{\text{Change in } y}{\text{Change in } x}$

The best way to find these two values is to draw in a triangle.

$m = \frac{5}{0.5}$ ✓

$\quad = 10$ ✓

b) Give an interpretation of the gradient. *(1 mark)*

Klaudia ran at 10 km per hour for the first half an hour of her run. ✓

Put the value you found in part **a)** into the context of the question.

4.6 Sequences

Sequences are seen in all areas of life. Among other things, they can be used to model the growth of plants, apply **interest** to bank loans or savings and create patterns in art.

Arithmetic Sequences

An **arithmetic sequence** is one which increases or decreases by a constant amount each time (this is called the common difference). Questions will usually have patterns or numbers to be continued.

Example 4.6.1

Anya is making mosaic patterns with hexagonal tiles as shown below. The number of tiles she uses each time forms an arithmetic sequence.

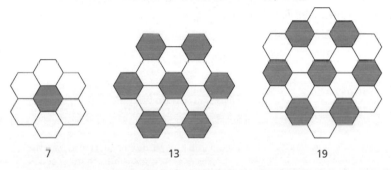

7   13   19

a)   Can Anya make a pattern with 100 tiles? Justify your answer. *(2 marks)*

In this question you will need to justify your answer. Just saying 'yes' or 'no' will not get any marks.

7   13   19
\ / \ /
6   6

nth term 6*n* + 1

$6n + 1 = 100$

$\quad -1 \quad -1$

$\dfrac{6n}{6} = \dfrac{99}{6}$

$n = \dfrac{33}{2}$ ✓

n is not an integer so 100 is not in the sequence. ✓

First find the *n*th term. Find the difference between the terms, which will then be multiplied by *n*. Then look for the difference between this and the first term and either add on or subtract the value.

Put the *n*th term equal to 100. If it is in the sequence, this will tell you which term it is.

State your conclusion clearly at the end.

b) Anya buys the tiles for 30p each. She spends £16.50 on tiles.

Which term in the sequence will this be? *(2 marks)*

$\frac{1650}{30}$ = 55 tiles used ✓

$6n + 1 = 55$

$-1 \quad -1$

$\frac{6n}{6} = \frac{54}{6}$

$n = 9$

The ninth term in the sequence will cost £16.50 ✓

> Start off by working out how many tiles are used. Remember to make sure the units are the same first.

> Put the nth term formula equal to the number of tiles and solve the equation.

c) Anya uses the formula $3 + 1.5n$ to decide how much to sell the mosaics for. She notices that this works well for small mosaics but she loses money on the larger pieces.

Which is the first term whereby Anya will lose money? *(3 marks)*

Cost of tiles in a mosaic is $0.3(6n + 1)$

$0.3(6n + 1) > 3 + 1.5n$

$\frac{0.3(6n + 1)}{0.3} > \frac{3 + 1.5n}{0.3}$ ✓

$6n + 1 > 10 + 5n$

$-5n -5n$

$n + 1 > 10$

$-1 \quad -1$

$n > 9$ ✓

The first she will lose money on is the tenth term. ✓

> Using the nth term, write a formula for the cost of the tiles.

> She will lose money when the cost of the tiles is greater than the price she is selling the mosaics for, so this can be written as an inequality.

> Solving the inequality shows that n must be greater than 9, so the tenth term will be the first to lose money. Make your answer clear at the end.

Fibonacci Sequences

Fibonacci was a mathematician at a time when studying mathematics was thought to be a dangerous thing to allow people to do. He wrote a lot about mathematics that was disguised as something else. The most famous example of this is the **Fibonacci sequence**, where he looked at how a population of rabbits would grow. This sequence is found throughout the natural world and creates some beautiful patterns. The sequence is formed by adding the previous two terms.

Example 4.6.2

Find the first term of a Fibonacci sequence in which the second term is 5 and the sixth term is 31. *(3 marks)*

Let the first term be x.

Term 1: x

Term 2: 5

Term 3: $x + 5$

Term 4: $5 + x + 5 = x + 10$ ✓

Term 5: $x + 5 + x + 10 = 2x + 15$ ✓

Term 6: $x + 10 + 2x + 15 = 3x + 25$

$3x + 25 = 31$

$$\begin{array}{r} -25 \quad -25 \\ \dfrac{3x}{3} = \dfrac{6}{3} \\ x = 2 \checkmark \end{array}$$

You haven't been told the first term, so it can be given a letter; this could be anything but x is the most obvious one to go for.

The terms can then be written out clearly to keep track of which term you are up to until you get to the sixth term.

Now you know the sixth term algebraically, you can put it equal to 31 to make an equation that can be solved.

Geometric Sequences

In a **geometric sequence**, each term is multiplied by a common ratio to get the next term. A typical question is given below and it demonstrates how quickly these sorts of sequences can grow.

Example 4.6.3

Yuen is saving money. The first week he saves £1, the second week he doubles this to save £2 and in the third week he doubles the amount again to save £4.

a) How much money in total will Yuen have saved in six weeks? *(3 marks)*

Week 1:	£1	Week 4:	£8	
Week 2:	£2	Week 5:	£16	✓
Week 3:	£4	Week 6:	£32	✓

$1 + 2 + 4 + 8 + 16 + 32 = £63$ ✓

Setting out the weeks clearly helps you to keep track of things.

b) Yuen plans to continue this savings plan for a year.
Do you think this is a good idea? *(1 mark)*

This is not a good idea as the amount he will need to save each week will quickly get very big and he is unlikely to be able to keep this up. ✓

You could of course answer 'yes' that he should continue with the savings plan for a year because he will have saved a lot of money; but you would have to assume he is very rich!

For more on the topics covered in this chapter, see pages 14–17, 42–45, 52–55, 76–81 & 104–105 of the Collins Edexcel Maths Foundation Revision Guide.

Algebra: Key Notes

- You should know how to tell if something is an expression, an equation, a formula, an inequality or an identity.
- To factorise a quadratic in the form $x^2 + bx + c$, look for two numbers that will multiply together to give c and add together to give b.
- Linear equations are solved by keeping both sides balanced, meaning that whatever you do to one side you should also do to the other.
- Inequalities are solved in the same way as equations, but if you multiply or divide by a negative you need to reverse the inequality sign.
- To solve a **quadratic equation**, you should factorise and then put each bracket equal to 0 to form simple linear equations, which you can then solve.
- On a graph, the midpoint of two coordinates can be found by adding together each of the coordinates and halving them, i.e. $\left(\frac{x_1 + x_2}{2}, \frac{y_1 + y_2}{2}\right)$
- The general equation of a straight line is $y = mx + c$, where m is the gradient and c is the y-intercept.
- Parallel lines have the same gradient.
- To find the gradient of a line, use $m = \frac{\text{Change in } y}{\text{Change in } x}$
- When finding the equation of a line, substitute the value of the gradient and a pair of coordinates into $y = mx + c$ to find the value of c.
- If asked to sketch a curve, ensure you include labels for all points of intersection with the axes. See page 138 for examples of different types of graph.
- A positive quadratic will be shaped like a smile and a negative will be shaped like a frown.
- To find the nth term in sequences, look for the common difference between the terms. n will be multiplied by this number. You then look at what must be added on or subtracted from this value to get the first term.
- In a Fibonacci sequence, the previous two terms are added together to find the next term.

5 Ratio, Proportion and Rates of Change

About 25% of the marks on the exam paper will be based on Ratio, Proportion and Rates of Change (RPRoC).

Ratio is used to compare the parts within the whole and proportion compares each part to the whole. If you consider that your exam paper will be 25% RPRoC, that is proportion as you are considering how much of the whole. However, you could also say that the paper will be 1 mark on RPRoC to every 3 marks on any other topic, giving a ratio of 1 : 3. You need to be comfortable changing between the different forms of expressing ratios and proportions.

Rates of change looks at the proportional increase, or decrease, to a population, value or quantity.

5.1 Scales – Maps, Models and Diagrams

Scales are often expressed as a ratio. The use of ratio means that there is no need for units of measurement (or that they can be used with any unit of measure). However, sometimes the ratio will be given in terms of 1 cm for every 5 m, or similar. You must ensure that your final answer makes sense and is in reasonable units. When establishing a scale factor or ratio between the model and real life, or the similar shapes, it is important to remember that the ratio between linear measurements is not the same as the ratio between the areas or the volumes.

Example 5.1

Harriet is making some toy dinosaurs. Each is a scale version of the real dinosaurs, based on current expert opinion.

Dinosaur Toy	Tyrannosaurus Rex	Giraffatitan	Triceratops	Stegosaurus
Length	15 cm	20 cm	11 cm	9 cm
Height	5.8 cm	11 cm	3.4 cm	3.9 cm

Each toy will have a tag with some key facts about the dinosaur attached to it. She has started writing the labels but cannot remember which toy each label belongs to.

Being asked to justify your answer means you need to support your answer with good mathematical steps. A paragraph isn't necessary but some words can help to explain what you are doing.

a) Match these labels to the right toy. Justify your answer. *(3 marks)*

Name:
Actual height: 2.8 m
Actual length: 9 m
Interesting fact:

A

Name:
Actual height: 5 m
Actual length: 13 m
Interesting fact:

B

Name:
Actual height: 3.5 m
Actual length: 8 m
Interesting fact:

C

Dinosaur Toy	Tyrannosaurus	Giraffatitan	Triceratops	Stegosaurus
Length	15 cm	20 cm	11 cm	9 cm
Height	5.8 cm	11 cm	3.4 cm	3.9 cm
Length ÷ Height	2.5862...	1.8181...	3.2352...	2.3076... ✓

A: Length ÷ Height = 9 ÷ 2.8 = 3.2142...
This most closely matches the triceratops toy's length to height ratio (3.2352...).
B: Length ÷ Height = 13 ÷ 5 = 2.6
This most closely matches the t-rex toy's length to height ratio (2.5862...).
C: Length ÷ Height = 8 ÷ 3.5 = 2.2857...
This most closely matches the stegosaurus toy's length to height ratio (2.3076...). ✓
Label A goes on the triceratops, B goes on the tyrannosaurus rex and C goes on the stegosaurus. ✓

The final label has been more fully completed.

Name: Giraffatitan
Actual height:
Actual length: 22 m
Interesting fact: From the Jurassic period this dino held the largest dino record until the Giant Titanosaurians claimed the lead along with the Sauroposeidon.

b) i) Express the scale, as a unit ratio, of the giraffatitan toy based on its label information. *(1 mark)*

Toy size : Actual size
20 cm : 22 m
20 : 2200
1 : 110 ✓

Be clear as to which way round you are establishing your ratio. Think whether there is a way that will make more sense or be neater if you are given a choice. Make sure that the units are the same.

ii) Find the missing height of the giraffatitan, rounded to the nearest half metre.
(2 marks)

The toy has a height of 11 cm. 11 × 110 = 1210 cm ✓ Height of actual giraffatitan = 12.0 m (to the nearest half metre) ✓	Always look out for the final answer form required by the question; in this case, round to the nearest half metre. 12.1 m is between 12.0 m and 12.5 m but closer to 12, so is rounded down.

5.2 Ratios

Ratios are a way of expressing quantities, such as for converting currencies or mixing colours of paint. There are lots of different ways you can be asked about ratio, some more obvious than others. Carefully consider what information the question gives and what you are trying to find.

Example 5.2

Jenny and Ted are making drinks of fruit juice. Jenny likes to have her juice diluted in a ratio of juice to water of 3 . 1. Ted likes his juice to water ratio to be 1 : 1. There is 240 ml of juice left.

a) Jenny and Ted share the juice equally.
What is the difference in volume of their drinks once diluted? *(3 marks)*

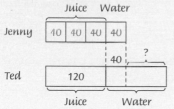

Each get 240 ml ÷ 2 = 120 ml of juice.

120 ÷ 3 = 40 ml   ← (each 'part' of
                              Jenny's drink) ✓

Jenny 40 × 4 = 160 ml;

Ted 120 × 2 = 240 ml ✓

240 − 160 = 80 ml so Ted gets 80 ml more drink. ✓

b) How much juice should they each start with so that the final volume of their drinks is equal? *(2 marks)*

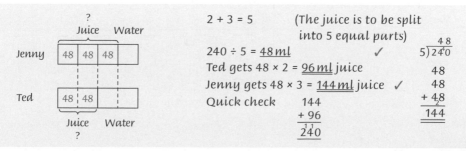

2 + 3 = 5   (The juice is to be split
                     into 5 equal parts)

240 ÷ 5 = 48 ml   ✓

Ted gets 48 × 2 = 96 ml juice

Jenny gets 48 × 3 = 144 ml juice ✓

Quick check   144
                  + 96
                  240

$$\begin{array}{r} 4\,8 \\ 5\overline{)2\,4\,^40} \\ 4\,8 \\ 4\,8 \\ +\,4\,8 \\ \hline 1\,4\,4 \end{array}$$

c) What fraction of Ted's drink is water? *(1 mark)*

$\frac{1}{2}$ ✓

> 1 : 1 means there are two parts altogether, of which one is water.

5.3 Ratios – Comparing and Calculating

Using unit ratios, or the form 1 : x, can be a good way to compare different ratios.

> To compare the ratios, you can turn them all into unit ratios (in the form 1 : x). To do this, divide both sides by the value of the left-hand side.

Example 5.3

An artist is mixing colours for her painting. She uses a mix of midnight-blue and white in a ratio of 5 : 2 to make a lighter blue. She now wants to make a slightly paler blue, to add highlights.

a) She chooses from these ratios for the slightly paler blue:

8 : 3   12 : 5   15 : 6

Which ratio should she use? *(3 marks)*

> Once expressed in a way that is easier to compare, you need to be careful about your interpretation. This question is asking for a lighter colour, which means that the amount of white for each part blue has to be higher.

5 : 2 *(divide both sides by 5)* ⇒ 1 : 0.4

8 : 3 *(divide both sides by 8)* ⇒ 1 : 0.375

12 : 5 *(divide both sides by 12)* ⇒ 1 : 0.41̇6̇ ✓

15 : 6 *(divide both sides by 15)* ⇒ 1 : 0.4 ✓

12 : 5 *is the ratio she should use.* ✓

$2 \div 5$

$\rightarrow \quad 5\overline{)2.0}^{0.4}$

$3 \div 8$

$\rightarrow \quad 8\overline{)3.^30^60^40}^{0.\ 3\ 7\ 5}$

$5 \div 12$

$\rightarrow \quad 12\overline{)5.0^20^80^80...}^{0.4\ 1\ 6\ 6...}$

$6 \div 15$

$\rightarrow \quad 15\overline{)6.0}^{0.4}$

b) The artist has lots of tubes of midnight-blue paint but only three tubes of white. She decides to use all of the white tubes of paint.
How much blue should she mix in to get the same paler colour as in part **a)**? *(2 marks)*

Blue : White

$\times \frac{3}{5}$ ⌒ 12 : 5 ⌒ $\times \frac{3}{5}$
      ⌄ x : 3 ⌄

> To find the **multiplier**, you can use the fact that division is the inverse operation. So $3 \div 5 = \frac{3}{5}$ gives the multiplier. This is then used to multiply both sides to find the equivalent ratio with three parts white.

$12 \times \frac{3}{5} = 12 \times 3 \div 5$ ✓

$= 36 \div 5$

$= 36 \times 2 \div 10$

$= 72 \div 10$

$= 7.2$

> Always check your answer makes sense and has units – in this case the units are 'tubes of paint'. 7.2 is a reasonable number but check if using a decimal makes sense in the context. In this case you can get 0.2 or one-fifth of a tube of paint.

She should mix in 7.2 tubes of blue paint to get the same colour. ✓

There are many ways of carrying out calculations without your calculator. It is up to you which method you use.

5.4 Compound Measure

Compound means a mixture of more than one measure. In this case, it is measures that are expressed as a combination of the standard base units. Pressure is Nm^{-2} or N/m^2. This is the force (measured in Newtons, N) divided by the area (measured in m^2). Dimensional analysis can be a very helpful way of supporting and checking your working. If your answer is in N/m^2, then to get there you must divide the force by the area.

Example 5.4

Speed is a measurement of distance divided by time. Joanna is travelling at a constant speed on the motorway and the sat-nav tells her that it is 6.5 miles to her exit. She says that this will take her 10 minutes as she is travelling at 65 mph. Is she correct? *(2 marks)*

$Speed = 65\,mph;$ Distance to go is 6.5 miles

$s = \frac{d}{t}$ so $t = \frac{d}{s}$

$t = \frac{6.5}{65} = 0.1\ hours$ ✓

$0.1 = \frac{1}{10} = 1 \div 10$

$60\ minutes \div 10 = 6\ minutes$

$t = 6\ minutes$

> When presented with a possible solution to a problem, you can be misled trying to follow the method used. Try starting with the elements of the problem and finding your own answer to compare.

Joanna is incorrect. It will take her 6 minutes to reach her exit travelling at 65 mph. ✓

5.5 Direct Proportion – Recipes

Recipes are often used as a way of looking at proportions. The recipe will work as long as the proportions of ingredients stay the same. If you use 100g flour for every egg, then for two eggs you would have 200g flour. If you only had 50g flour, you would use half an egg. There is also lots of possibility for unit conversions too, so watch out!

Example 5.5

Gerald is baking some buns for a cake sale at school. Gerald wants to make as many buns as he can with the ingredients he already has. He knows that $1\,oz \approx 28\,g$, and 1 pint = 32 tablespoons.

Gerald has:
- Plenty of food colouring and vanilla extract
- 1.5 kg of butter
- $1\frac{1}{2}$ bags of self-raising flour (500 g when full)
- $\frac{3}{4}$ of a bag of caster sugar (1 kg when full)
- 2 kg of icing sugar
- $\frac{1}{2}$ pint of milk
- A dozen free-range eggs

To make 12 buns:
4 oz butter or margarine
4 oz self-raising flour
3 oz caster sugar
1 tsp vanilla extract
$1\frac{1}{2}$ tbsp milk
2 free-range eggs, lightly beaten

For the buttercream icing
5 oz butter, softened
10 oz icing sugar
1.5 tbsp milk
A few drops of food colouring

a) Complete the table to find the greatest number of buns Gerald can make whilst using a whole number of eggs. *(5 marks)*

INGREDIENTS	For 12 buns Gerald needs			For one bun	He has	Enough for how many buns?
	In ounces	Calculation	Amount			
Butter						
Self-raising flour	4	4 × 28	112 g	$112 \div 12$ $= 9\frac{1}{3}$ g	750 g	$750 \div 9\frac{1}{3}$ $= 80.357...$
Caster sugar						
Icing sugar						
Milk						
Eggs						

> There are lots of ways to be clear in your working. Tables can help set out working where there is a process repeated a number of times.

> It doesn't matter if you convert the recipe into grams or the ingredient list into ounces. The numbers will be different but the theory is the same.

INGREDIENTS	For 12 buns Gerald needs			For one bun	He has	Enough for how many buns?
	In ounces	Calculation	Amount			
Butter	4 + 5 = 9	9 × 28	252 g	$252 \div 12$ $= 21$ g	1500 g	$1500 \div 21$ $= 71.428...$
Self-raising flour	4	4 × 28	112 g	$112 \div 12$ $= 9\frac{1}{3}$ g	750 g	$750 \div 9\frac{1}{3}$ $= 80.357...$
Caster sugar	3	3 × 28	84 g	$84 \div 12 =$ 7 g	750 g	$750 \div 7$ $= 107.142...$
Icing sugar	10	10 × 28	280 g	$280 \div 12$ $= 23\frac{1}{3}$ g	2000 g	$2000 \div 23\frac{1}{3}$ $= 85.714...$
Milk		1.5 + 1.5	3 tbsp	$3 \div 12 =$ $\frac{1}{4}$ tbsp	$0.5 \times 32 =$ 16 tbsp	$16 \div \frac{1}{4}$ $= 64$
Eggs			2 eggs	$\frac{1}{6}$ egg	12 eggs	$12 \div \frac{1}{6}$ $= 72$ ✓✓

Buns Gerald can make (b)

$b \leq 64$ (as he is limited by milk) ✓

Each whole egg makes 6 buns so Gerald can make 60 buns using a whole number of eggs. ✓ ✓

If you spot a shortcut, such as looking at multiples of half the recipe (which works in this case as that is for each whole egg), then you can use it. The method of finding one 'bun', then multiplying up, will work in all cases; but you need to remember to consider the number of whole eggs at the end.

b) When baking, 15% of the buns get burned and are thrown away. Gerald ices the rest of the buns in purple and red in a ratio of 8 : 9. He sells the purple buns in bundles of three for 50p and the red buns individually for 20p each.

If Gerald manages to sell all his buns, how much money will he have made? *(4 marks)*

A question like this can seem overwhelming. Break it up into parts. If the question asked you to find 15% of 60, it would make for an easy start. Part of the skill is recognising what you need to do. Even if you cannot get all the marks, it is important to get some of the method marks.

60 buns go into the oven

15% of 60 = 6 + 3 = 9

60 − 9 = 51 (buns to be sold) ✓

Ratio 8 : 9

8 + 9 = 17

51 ÷ 17 = 3

Purple : Red

8 × 3 : 9 × 3

24 : 27   (Check 24 + 27 = 51) ✓

Income from purple buns is 24 ÷ 3 = 8

8 × 0.50 = £4 ✓

Income from red buns is 27 × 0.20 = £5.40

Total income = 4 + 5.40 = £9.40 ✓

Working:

10% of 60 = 6

5% of 60 = 3

15% = 3 + 6

85% = 100% − 15%

= 60 − 9 = 51

Purple : Red

8 : 9

8 + 9 = 17 so there are 17 parts altogether.

To share 51 into 17 parts you divide. 51 ÷ 17

He will make 24 purple buns and 27 red buns.

5.6 Fractions and Percentages

You need to be able to interpret fractions of quantities and represent quantities as fractions. Being able to simplify your fractions and convert from mixed numbers to improper (top-heavy) fractions are key skills. Keep the context in mind and check that your answer seems sensible.

A fraction can be greater than 1 but at other times this wouldn't make sense (for example in probability). You need to be able to represent fractions as percentages too. As with fractions, there are times when a value of more than 100% wouldn't make sense and other times when it is perfectly acceptable. Consider the context.

Example 5.6

Martin grows potatoes. In the first year he harvests 54 potatoes. In the second year he harvests 66 potatoes.

a) What is his yield in the second year as a fully simplified fraction of his harvest in the first year? *(2 marks)*

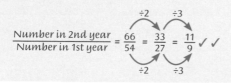

$$\frac{\text{Number in 2nd year}}{\text{Number in 1st year}} = \frac{66}{54} = \frac{33}{27} = \frac{11}{9} \checkmark \checkmark$$

b) In the third year, Martin harvests 60 potatoes. He says that as this is 111% (to the nearest whole percent) of the potatoes he grew in the first year, then it is 89% of the potatoes he grew in the second year (since 60 is exactly between 54 and 66).

Is Martin correct? *(4 marks)*

$60 \div 54 \times 100 = 111.1111... \checkmark$

So Martin is correct that 60 is 111% of 54. $\checkmark$

$60 \div 66 \times 100 = 90.909090... \checkmark$

So Martin is incorrect that it is 89% of the potatoes he grew in the second year. It is actually 90.9% of the potatoes he grew in the second year. $\checkmark$

In this case, Martin's mistake is that what represents 100% is different in each case. If he was comparing each of the first two years to the third year (100%), then it is true that there would be the same difference in percentage. He is comparing first to year 1 being 100%, then to year 3 being 100%. So in this case he is wrong.

If you are asked to consider someone else's working, try to do the question yourself. See what you get independently so you don't get confused by their possible mistakes.

5.7 Percentage Increase and Decrease

There are many key words associated with growth and decay. You need to recognise them and understand them. **Depreciation** means a decrease in the value and decay tends to mean a decrease in the quantity (generally given as a percentage). Interest means an increase in value and growth means an increase in the quantity (for example in population size).

Example 5.7

Jaden bought a brand new car. In the first year it depreciated by 38%. He predicts that after this initial drop, it will depreciate steadily at a rate of 12.5% each year.

a) Jaden says that, as 38 + 12.5 = 50.5%, after the second year the value of the car will be just under half its original value.
Is Jaden correct? You must give a reason for your answer. *(2 marks)*

> Jaden is incorrect as the 12.5% is only applied to the value of the car at the start of the second year. ✓
>
> The car retains 62% of its value in year 1. It retains 87.5% of the value in the second year.
>
> $0.62 \times 0.875 = 0.5425 = 54.25\%$ of the original value at the end of the second year. ✓
>
> His car will be worth over half its original value.

A common mistake is to add the percentage values.

b) After one year, the value of the car is £10155. Jaden decides to sell it when the value is less than £7000.
After how many <u>more</u> years will Jaden sell the car? *(3 marks)*

> $1.00 - 0.125 = 0.875$
>
> After 1 more year: $10155 \times 0.875^1 = 8885.625$ ✓
>
> After 2 more years: $10155 \times 0.875^2 = 7774.921875$ ✓
>
> After 3 more years: $10155 \times 0.875^3 = 6803.05664...$
>
> Jaden will sell the car after three more years. ✓

Find your decimal multiplier. 0.125 is the decimal equivalent to 12.5%.

Calculator shortcut: many calculators will let you scroll back into the first calculation and change the numbers, which saves keying it all in again. Get to know your calculator!

5.8 Reverse Percentages

Finding a **percentage increase** or **decrease** is important, but if you can do something one way you need to be able to reverse it. Finding original values, or reverse percentage calculations, often catch students out as they treat the value given as 100% and add, or subtract, the percentage change. Remember that if you know how to add or subtract a percentage, it gives you a way to check your final answer. Think about what you would do if you were finding the 'sale' value and then carry out the opposite.

Example 5.8

A sports shop is having a '25% off sale' to clear old stock.

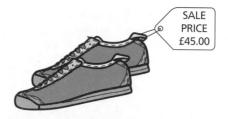

SALE PRICE £45.00

a)   A pair of trainers costs £45.00 in the sale. What would the trainers have cost before the sale? *(3 marks)*

45 = 75% of original value ✓

45 ÷ 75 = 0.6 (1% of the original value) ✓

Original value = 0.6 × 100 = £60 ✓

In this part of the question, the method used is to find what the sale price is equivalent to. Then use that to find 1% of the original value and multiply by 100.

If items haven't sold after the sale has run for a week, they have a further reduction.

b)   A badminton racket cost £56.25 in the 25% off sale. After a week, it is reduced to £45.00.

What is the percentage reduction in the new sale from the original pre-sale price? *(4 marks)*

56.25 = 0.75 × Pre-sale price ✓

Pre-sale price = 56.25 ÷ 0.75 = £75 ✓

New sale price is £45.

$\frac{45}{75}$ × 100 = 60, so the sale price is 60% of the pre-sale price. ✓

100 − 60 = 40

The new sale is 40% off. ✓

If you are used to decimal multipliers and were asked to find a reduction of 25%, you would multiply by 0.75. So to do the inverse, you divide by 0.75.

5.9 Direct Proportion

In **direct proportion**, one element increases by the same proportion as another. So if one value doubles, the other also doubles. If y is proportional to x, then if y doubles the value of x also doubles.

Example 5.9

Ellen is designing a garden path.
The graph shows the relationship between the length of the path in metres and the cost of materials to make it.

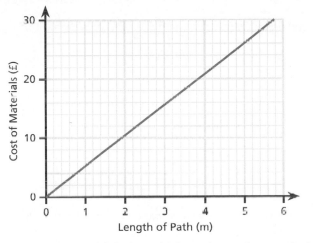

a) How much would the materials cost to make a path that is 5 m long? *(1 mark)*

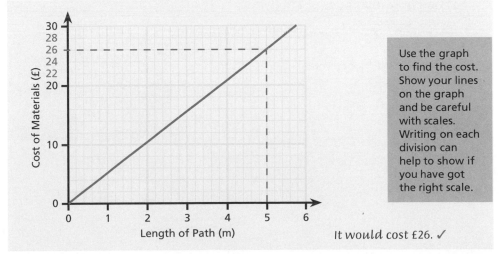

Use the graph to find the cost. Show your lines on the graph and be careful with scales. Writing on each division can help to show if you have got the right scale.

It would cost £26. ✓

Ratio, Proportion and Rates of Change

b) Ellen uses the equation $F = 120 + 5.5x$ to calculate her fee in pounds for the work, where x is the length of the path.

i) Ellen charges a set fee for the design then a small amount per metre for doing the work. What is her set fee? *(1 mark)*

Her set fee is £120. ✓

If the path was 0 metres long, she would charge £120 as $120 + 5.5 \times 0 = 120$.

ii) How much does Ellen charge per metre of path? *(1 mark)*

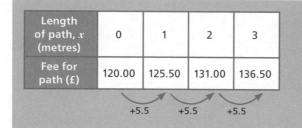

Ellen charges £5.50 per metre of path. ✓

iii) Ellen builds a path that is 9 m long. How much money will she be left with after paying for materials? *(4 marks)*

Materials cost per metre is $C = kx$

$26 = k \times 5$

$k = \frac{26}{5} = 5.2$ ✓

Materials cost £5.20 per metre.

$5.2 \times 9 = 46.80$ ✓

Total fee for the path is

$F = 120 + 5.5x$

$F = 120 + 5.5 \times 9 = £169.50$ ✓

$169.50 - 46.80 = £122.70$

Ellen will be left with £122.70 ✓

Another method you could use is to say that the money she is left with is
$120 + 0.30x$
$120 + 0.3 \times 9 = 120 + 2.70$
$\qquad\qquad\qquad = 122.70$

5.10 Inverse Proportion

Inverse proportion is when as one variable increases, the other variable decreases. If x is inversely proportional to y, the relationship is:

$x \propto \dfrac{1}{y} \rightarrow x = \dfrac{k}{y}$, where k is a **constant**.

Example 5.10

The **cross-sectional** area of a fixed length of wire is inversely proportional to its resistance. When the area of the wire is 0.125 mm², the resistance is 60 Ω.

a) What would be the resistance if the wire had a cross-sectional area of 0.2 mm²?
    (3 marks)

$R \propto \dfrac{1}{A}$

$R = \dfrac{k}{A}$ ✓

Using the given situation to find k.

$k = R \times A$

$\quad = 60 \times 0.125 = 7.5$ ✓

> k is a constant so has no units.

Using k to find the new situation with R:

$R = \dfrac{7.5}{0.2} = 37.5\,\Omega$ ✓

b) What must be the cross-sectional area of the wire to have a resistance of 15 Ω?
    (3 marks)

$R = \dfrac{k}{A}$

*From part **a)** $k = 7.5$ and from the question $R = 15$*

$15 = \dfrac{7.5}{A}$ ✓

$15A = 7.5$ ✓

$A = \dfrac{7.5}{15} = 0.5\,mm^2$ ✓

> You can either rearrange algebraically, to make R the subject of the formula, or you can substitute in the values you know, then solve from there.

> 15 Ω is a lower resistance than the others, so you would expect the wire to have a larger cross-sectional area. By checking this is true for your answer, you are more likely to spot mistakes and be able to correct them.

5.11 Compound Interest

Interest is a term related to monetary values. You will come across interest as part of saving and borrowing money.

Example 5.11

Sian puts £100 in her bank account at the start of the year. Her bank pays **compound interest** of 2.5% per annum on all savings.

a) How much money will Sian have after one year? *(1 mark)*

> 1% of £100 = £1
>
> 2.5% = £1 × 2.5 = £2.5
>
> Interest is increase, so after 1 year she will have £102.50. ✓

b) How much money will Sian have after five years? *(3 marks)*

> 100% is the original amount.
>
> 100% + 2.5% = 102.5% ✓
>
> As a decimal = 1.025 (this is the decimal multiplier)
>
> $100 × 1.025^5 = 113.1408... = £113.14$ ✓ ✓

You can do the calculations for each year at a time but it is easier to use a decimal multiplier, especially when there are so many years. The key is finding the decimal multiplier.

5.12 Growth and Decay

Growth and decay are used to describe proportional increases and decreases in non-monetary values. A good example is if you were looking at population change. You may have also come across the idea in science, when looking at carbon dating for example. The methods used are the same as for interest and depreciation but the words used to describe it are different. See the Glossary on page 139.

Example 5.12

The population of foxes in a five-mile radius from Lucy's home is 423. The population is growing at a rate of 2% each year.

a) How many foxes will there be after one year? *(2 marks)*

> Decimal multiplier = 1 + 0.02 = 1.02 ✓
>
> 423 × 1.02 = 431.46
>
> After one year there will be 431 foxes (to the nearest whole fox). ✓

The population of rabbits in the same area is decaying at a rate of 7%.

b) After one year there are 5432 rabbits.
How many were there at the start of the year? *(3 marks)*

$1 - 0.07 = 0.93$ ✓

$x \times 0.93 = 5432$ ✓

$x = 5432 \div 0.93 = 5841$ ✓

A potential mistake here is missing that it is a reverse percentage question. You are asked to find an original amount, so you need to find your decimal multiplier and then divide by it.

c) What will be the joint population of rabbits and foxes after a further three years? *(3 marks)*

Population of rabbits after a further three years is $5432 \times 0.93^3 = 4369.267224$ ✓

Population of foxes after a further three years is $431 \times 1.02^3 = 457.380648$ ✓

Joint population is $4369 + 457 = 4826$ ✓

d) Assume that in one night at the start of the second year, every fox caught and ate one rabbit.
What fraction of the rabbit population would have been eaten? *(2 marks)*

There are 5432 rabbits and 431 foxes, so 431 rabbits would have been eaten.

$\frac{431}{5432}$ ✓ ✓

This is a calculator question and most calculators give answers as simplified fractions. Make sure you know if your calculator does this. If not, see if you can simplify the fraction (you won't always be able to).

5.13 Graphical Representation of Proportionality

Proportionality (both direct and inverse) can be represented using graphs. You could be asked to convert currency using a graph. You need to be able to recognise what the graph for each relationship would look like and be able to interpret values.

Example 5.13

The graph shows the relationship between the base of a triangle (x) and its height (y), given a constant area (A).

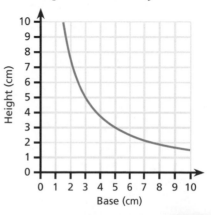

a) **i)** What is the height when the base length is 3 cm? *(1 mark)*

At $x = 3$, $y = 5\,cm$ ✓

ii) What is the area of the triangle? *(1 mark)*

So $A = \frac{1}{2}xy$

$\quad = \frac{1}{2} \times x \times y$

$\quad = \frac{1}{2} \times 3 \times 5 = 7.5\,cm^2$ ✓

b) What is the relationship between x and y in this situation? *(1 mark)*

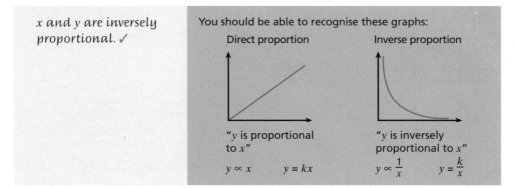

x and y are inversely proportional. ✓

You should be able to recognise these graphs:

Direct proportion

"y is proportional to x"

$y \propto x \qquad y = kx$

Inverse proportion

"y is inversely proportional to x"

$y \propto \frac{1}{x} \qquad y = \frac{k}{x}$

5.14 Compound Measures and Ratios

Questions will often expect you to decide which methods to use. Planning is important. Paying attention to the units can help if you get stuck with compound measures. If speed is measured in miles per hour, it is distance (miles) 'divided by' (per) time (hours).

Example 5.14

Jirair has a cuboid of copper.
Copper has a density of 8.96 g/cm³.
The ratio of the length to width to height of the cuboid is 5 : 1 : 3.
The height of the cuboid is 6 cm.

> Don't be put off by information that looks quite complicated. Often, if you start with something that you know, it can make everything a lot clearer.

What is the mass of Jirair's copper cuboid? Give your answer in kilograms to 3 significant figures. *(4 marks)*

5 : 1 : 3
? : ? : 6   ×2
10 : 2 : 6 ✓

> As ever, there are different ways to approach this question. Be clear and as long as your method is reasonable, you will get the marks.

Volume of the cuboid = 10 × 2 × 6 = 120 cm³ ✓
Mass of cuboid = 8.96 × 120
             = 1075.2 g ✓
             = 1.0752 kg = 1.08 kg (3 s.f.) ✓

> Is this the final answer? Is it in the required form?

5.15 Rate of Change at Point on Graph

The gradient of a graph is the rate of change. If the graph is curved, then the rate of change is itself changing but you can find the instantaneous rate of change as the gradient at that point. If the graph is linear, the rate of change is constant.

Example 5.15

A car is travelling along a straight track. The graph shows the velocity against time for the journey.

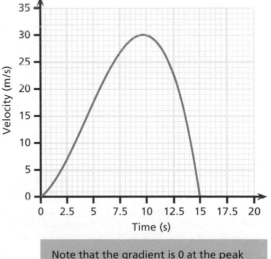

> Note that the gradient is 0 at the peak of the curve.

Acceleration is the rate of change of velocity against time.

a) At approximately what time is the acceleration of the car 0 m/s²? *(1 mark)*

The gradient is 0 and therefore the acceleration is 0 at $t \approx 9.7\,s$ ✓	The gradient of a curve is the rate of change of the velocity with regard to time, or acceleration. The acceleration is 0 m/s² when the gradient is 0. It is an approximation as it requires you to read the value from the graph. The accurate value is 9.6978… but you could never read a graph that accurately. It clearly falls between 9.5 and 10 though, so a value in this range is acceptable.

b) The line shows the **tangent** at $t = 5$.
Use this to estimate the acceleration at $t = 5$ s. *(3 marks)*

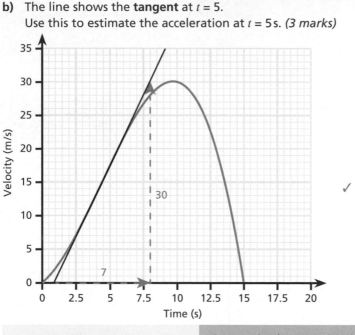

The gradient of the line at $t = 5$ s is: $\frac{30}{7} = 4.2857…$ ✓ $= 4.3\,m/s^2$ (2 s.f.) ✓	Once again, the approximation is because you need to read a value from the graph. The accurate answer would be 4.25 but it is impossible to get this accuracy when drawing on the gradient line and then reading values from it.

Whilst the question doesn't ask for a suitable degree of accuracy, it is good practice to round your final answer, especially when approximating. Show the more accurate value before rounding and say how you have rounded it.

For more on the topics covered in this chapter, see pages 18–21 of the Collins Edexcel Maths Foundation Revision Guide.

Ratio, Proportion and Rates of Change: Key Notes

- Ratios are used to consider components in comparison to each other. A ratio of 2 : 3 means that, for every two parts of the first thing, there are three parts of the second thing, with all parts being equal.
- A unit ratio is expressed as 1 : n. This form can be useful for comparing ratios.
- If you are looking at the proportion from the ratio 2 : 3, there are two red parts (for example) out of a total of five parts, giving $\frac{2}{5}$ red.
- Proportion looks at the part as compared to the whole, expressed as fractions, decimals or percentages.
- If you are sharing into a ratio, add up all the parts and divide to find out the value of each part. Then multiply up to find the value for each person or thing.
- Be careful – ratio and proportion questions may catch you out. They can be given in a strange context, asking you to find the total from one part or two parts, including algebra, etc.
- You can do quick checks on your working as you go along (e.g. add the final ratio to check the total is what it should be) to help avoid 'silly' calculation errors.
- Quantities are proportional when they increase or decrease at the same rate as each other. $y \propto x \rightarrow y = kx$
- Inverse proportion is when one quantity increases and the other decreases proportionally (i.e. if one doubles, the other halves). $y \propto \frac{1}{x} \rightarrow y = \frac{k}{x}$
- Interest is a proportional increase. If it is compound interest, the same interest is applied repeatedly (note that the second time the interest is applied, it is to the original amount and the interest from the first 'year'). For example £100 with 10% per annum compound interest ('per annum' means every year):

  After 1st year £110   After 2nd year £121   After 3rd year £133.10
- Using decimal multipliers is an efficient way to calculate repeated increases (interest/growth) and repeated decreases (depreciation/decay).
  - To find the decimal multiplier, find the decimal equivalent of the increase (consider it to be a negative increase for depreciation) and then add it to 1. Alternatively consider what percentage you will have after applying the interest once, then turn it into a decimal. To increase by 12% would be a multiplier of 1.12. To decrease by 7.6% would be a multiplier of 0.924.
- The use of algebra and graphs can take questions to a higher level when looking at proportionality. You need to be able to recognise these graphs:

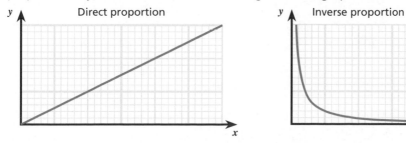

Geometry and Measures

Geometry has been a cornerstone of mathematics for thousands of years. The Ancient Greeks used geometrical proofs, where today you might choose to use algebra. The Egyptians used certain properties in building the pyramids, for example the properties of Pythagorean triples in order to create right angles.

6.1 Constructions and Loci

Loci are a set of points that obey a particular rule. You are often required to use construction methods to represent them. Remember that whenever you complete a construction, you need to leave in all your construction marks. They should be faint but visible so it is clear that you have followed the correct technique.

Example 6.1

Bill has a goat in a rectangular field, ABCD. He ties it to point H on a rectangular shed with a rope that is 2.2 m long, attached 1.5 m above the horizontal ground.

The goat can reach the ground 30 cm further than the length of the rope.

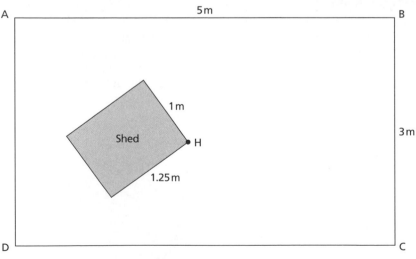

Scale: 2 cm = 1 m

a) What is the furthest horizontal distance that the goat can reach along the ground from point H? *(2 marks)*

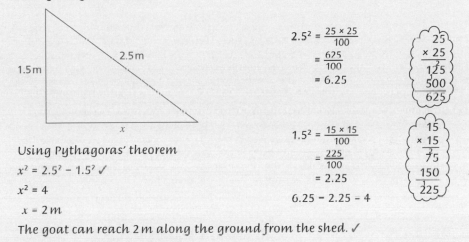

The goat can reach 30 cm + 2.2 m = 2.5 m from the point on the shed to the end of the goat's nose.

$2.5^2 = \frac{25 \times 25}{100}$

$= \frac{625}{100}$

$= 6.25$

```
   25
 × 25
  125
  500
  625
```

$1.5^2 = \frac{15 \times 15}{100}$

$= \frac{225}{100}$

$= 2.25$

$6.25 - 2.25 = 4$

```
   15
 × 15
   75
  150
  225
```

Using Pythagoras' theorem

$x^2 = 2.5^2 - 1.5^2$ ✓

$x^2 = 4$

$x = 2\,m$

The goat can reach 2 m along the ground from the shed. ✓

Bill wants to plant some trees along the perimeter of the field.
Each tree must be planted within 0.5 m of the perimeter fence.
Bill wants the trees to be closer to the fence AB than to BC.
If the goat can reach the trees when they are little she will eat them, so Bill will plant the trees out of the goat's reach.

b) Shade the region where Bill should plant his trees. *(7 marks)*

There are three separate constructions to consider here.

Constructing a line 0.5 m inside the fence: Measure 1 cm (represents 0.5 m) along each of the edges of the field and make a small mark, then join up faintly. This gives you a smaller, inner rectangle with some squares in each corner. Still using your ruler, go over the smaller rectangle.

Constructing an angle bisector of ABC: Construct two faint **arcs** an equal distance from B on BA and BC. Re-centre your compasses on each arc where it crosses the line (at each intersection). Draw a faint arc roughly where you expect the line to go, equal distance from each intersection. To do this, it is important to keep the compasses set the same. These should produce a cross and you can then use your ruler to draw the line through B and the cross all the way across the field.

Constructing the region reachable by the goat: The goat can reach 2 m along the ground. Faintly extend the lines of the shed away from H. Set your compasses to 4 cm (2 m). Draw an arc that goes from one faint line to the other. When the goat reaches the corner of the shed, the rope is effectively shorter. You can calculate the new length, or set your compasses by placing the point on the corner of the shed and matching the pencil to the arc where it meets the faint line. Use this to draw the arc until it meets the shed again.

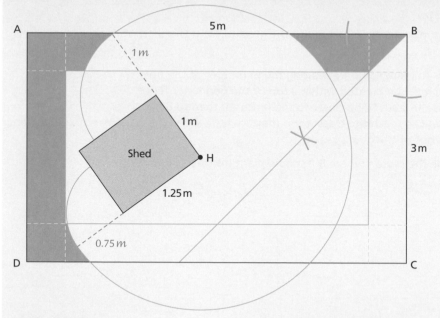

Mark allocation:

Angle bisector ABC. ✓ ✓
Rectangle construction. ✓
Large arc with radius 2 m. ✓

Small arcs with radius 1 m and
0.75 m respectively. ✓ ✓
Correct area shaded that meets
all criteria. ✓

6.2 Interior Angles

You should know how to find the **interior** (inside) and **exterior** (outside) **angles** of any **polygon**.

Example 6.2

A regular shape has an exterior angle of 24°.

a) How many edges does the shape have? *(2 marks)*

360 ÷ 24 = 15
✓

The shape has 15 edges. ✓

The sum of exterior angles is 360°.

b) What is the sum of the interior angles? *(2 marks)*

An interior angle = 180   24 = 156° ✓
Sum of interior angles = 15 × 156 = 2340° ✓

Regular means all the interior (and exterior) angles are equal.

6.3 Angle Properties and Reasoning

You are expected to be able to reason your answers when it comes to angle properties. Short sentences that have the name of the property and the logic behind it, alongside clear steps of working out, will show you understand and can communicate the understanding clearly.

Example 6.3

Find the values of x and y. State clearly the reasoning for each stage of your calculation.
(3 marks)

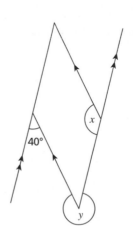

Diagram not to scale

As always there are different methods. Whatever your method, you won't get the marks for each step without explaining what you are doing and why.

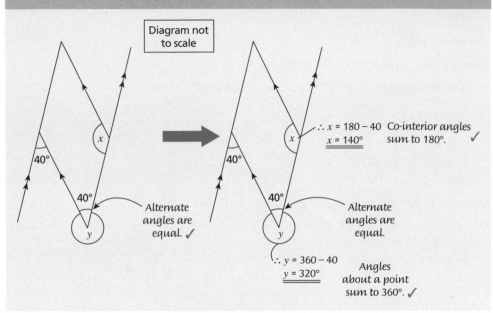

Diagram not to scale

$\therefore x = 180 - 40$ Co-interior angles
$x = 140°$ sum to 180°. ✓

Alternate angles are equal. ✓

Alternate angles are equal.

$\therefore y = 360 - 40$ Angles about a point sum to 360°. ✓
$y = 320°$

6.4 Quadrilaterals and Coordinate Axes

Quadrilaterals are polygons with four edges. You need to know the key properties of the following quadrilaterals: square, rectangle, parallelogram, trapezium, kite and rhombus. Coordinate axes are used as a way of describing two-dimensional space.

Example 6.4 📱

Evren has drawn some quadrilaterals.

He wants to plot them on coordinate axes. He has started finding the coordinates of one of the quadrilaterals:
A (–3, 1); B (6, 3); D (–4, –3). C lies on the *y*-axis.

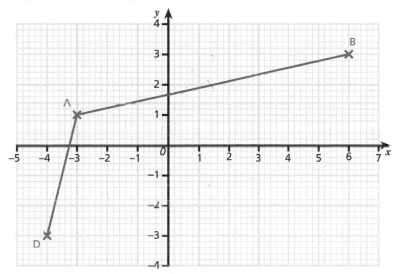

Find the name and dimensions of the quadrilateral. Justify each stage of your answer.
(8 marks)

**Possible
construction
method:**

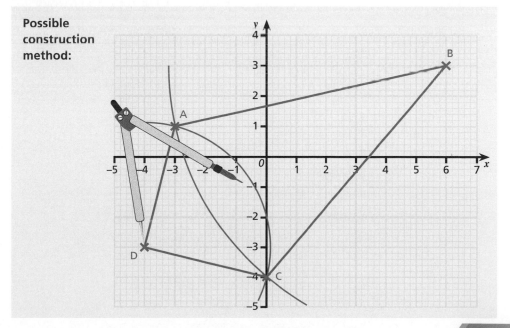

Possible algebra method:

Angle DAB is greater than 90° so it isn't a rectangle.

If it was a parallelogram then C would be 4 down and 1 left from B = (5, −1), which isn't on the y-axis, so it must be a kite. ✓ ✓

C (0, y)

As AD ≠ AB

AD = CD

AB = BC

To find the length of a line

$$\sqrt{(x_1 - x_2)^2 + (y_1 - y_2)^2}$$

As is often the case, there are many ways of doing this question. You could, for example, use the construction method shown on page 75 to find the missing vertex. This answer takes an algebraic approach but as long as you justify your working and show your method clearly, it is no better or worse than any other method.

$$AD = CD$$

When using this equation, it doesn't matter which way round you decide to use the x value for A and the x value for D, but it should be consistent with which way round you use the y values.

$$\sqrt{(x_A - x_D)^2 + (y_A - y_D)^2} = \sqrt{(x_C - x_D)^2 + (y_C - y_D)^2}$$
$$\sqrt{(-3 - -4)^2 + (1 - -3)^2} = \sqrt{(0 - -4)^2 + (y - -3)^2}$$
$$(-3 - -4)^2 + (1 - -3)^2 = (0 - -4)^2 + (y - -3)^2$$
$$1^2 + 4^2 = 4^2 + (y - -3)^2$$
$$1^2 = (y - -3)^2$$
$$y + 3 = \pm 1$$
$$\underline{y = -2 \text{ or } y = -4} \checkmark$$

$$AB = BC$$

$$\sqrt{(x_A - x_B)^2 + (y_A - y_B)^2} = \sqrt{(x_C - x_B)^2 + (y_C - y_B)^2}$$
$$\sqrt{(-3 - 6)^2 + (1 - 3)^2} = \sqrt{(0 - 6)^2 + (y - 3)^2}$$
$$(-9)^2 + (-2)^2 = (-6)^2 + (y - 3)^2$$
$$85 = 36 + (y - 3)^2$$
$$49 = (y - 3)^2$$
$$y - 3 = \pm 7$$
$$\underline{y = 10 \text{ or } -4} \checkmark$$

It would be very easy here to lose an answer. If it is a quadratic that you are solving, there will be two answers. If you only get one, you should check your working. It is possible to have no answers but if you have found one, then there should be a second one too.

Compare with answers above. y = −4 as it is true for both cases. ✓

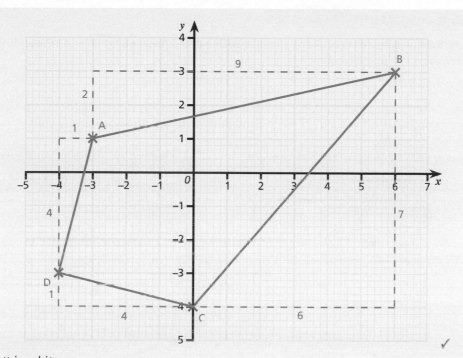

It is a kite.

$AB = BC = \sqrt{9^2 + 2^2} = \sqrt{85}$ ✓

$AD = CD = \sqrt{1^2 + 4^2} = \sqrt{17}$ ✓

Having two different ways of finding your answer can be useful. If questions don't specify a method, you can choose but don't spend too much time deliberating. Try something and if it doesn't seem to be working, try something else.

6.5 Congruent Triangles

Congruent shapes are exactly the same as each other. That means their corresponding dimensions and angles match.

Example 6.5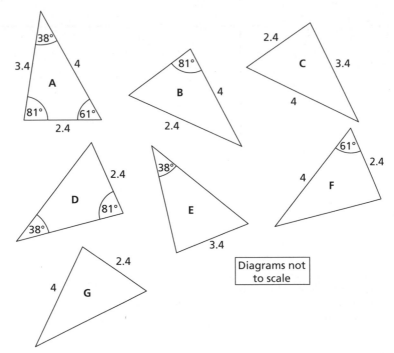

Determine if triangles B, C, D, E, F and G are congruent with triangle A, not congruent with triangle A, or if you do not have enough information to know. Justify your answers. *(4 marks)*

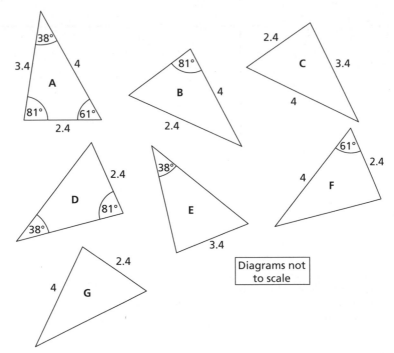

Diagrams not to scale

Triangle B is not congruent as the side opposite the 81° would need to be 4, not 2.4.

Triangle C is congruent (SSS).

Triangle D is congruent (AAS). ✓

Triangle E is not congruent as the side opposite the 38° would need to be 2.4, not 3.4. ✓

Triangle F is congruent (SAS). ✓

Triangle G: it is impossible to tell with only two pieces of information. ✓

One mark would be lost for each incorrect answer or missing justification.

6.6 Transformations (including Fractional Scale Factors)

Transformations include **rotations**, **reflections**, **translations** and **enlargements**.
Marks are often lost by certain elements of the question being ignored. Centres of rotation and lines of symmetry often require you to have a sound understanding of coordinates and equations of straight lines.

Example 6.6 📠

Two hexagons, A and B, are shown on the axes.

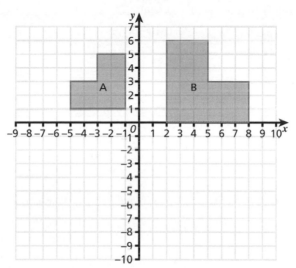

a) Reflect A in the line $y = -2$ and label the new shape, C. *(1 mark)*

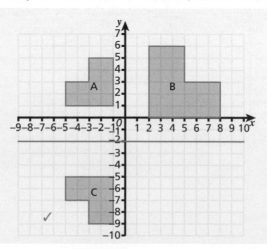

b) Rotate C 180° about (–1, –4). Label your new shape, D. *(2 marks)*

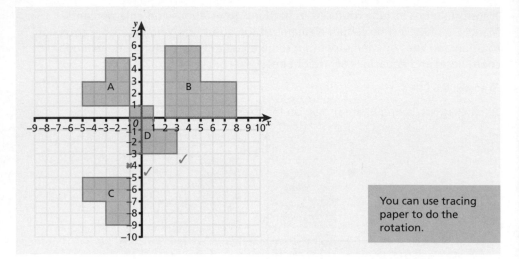

You can use tracing paper to do the rotation.

c) Describe fully the single transformation that maps D on to B. *(2 marks)*

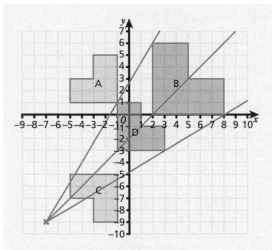

To find the **centre of enlargement**, join corresponding points on the two shapes. Where these lines cross is the centre of enlargement.

To find the scale factor:
Height of B = 6
Height of D = 4

$$4 \xrightarrow{\times ?} 6$$
$6 ÷ 4 = 1.5$
∴ Scale factor = 1.5

Describe <u>fully</u> the <u>single</u> transformation. Marks are often lost by students missing part of the description or describing it in more than one step.

An enlargement of scale factor 1.5, centre (–7, –9). ✓ ✓

6.7 Perimeter and Area of Compound Shapes

Perimeter is the distance around the outside of a shape. In practical terms, it might be needed to consider fencing or used to help find the surface area of a prism. The perimeter can be found by adding edges. The perimeter of a circle has a special name, circumference, and is found using the formula πd or $2\pi r$.

Area is the two-dimensional space within a shape. With a compound shape, the key is spotting the individual shapes which make it up and adding their areas to find the total for the compound shape.

Example 6.7

Sabiha is making scenery for a school play. A shape is formed using rectangles, a triangle and a semicircle, as shown in the diagram.

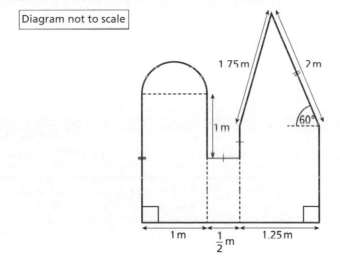

Diagram not to scale

Before painting the piece of scenery, Sabiha sticks tape along the edges to protect against splinters.

a) How many full metres of tape will Sabiha need to cover all the edges? *(5 marks)*

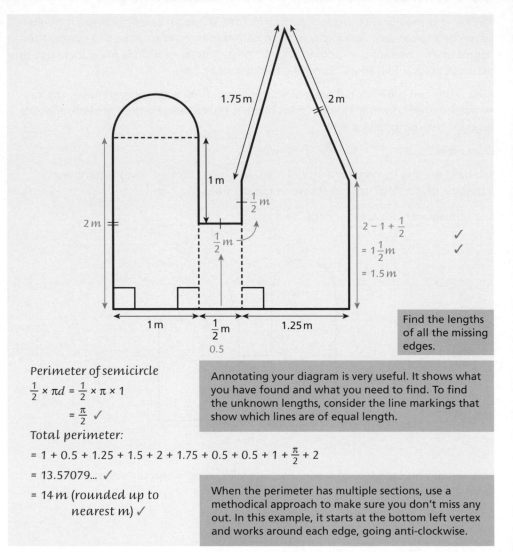

Find the lengths of all the missing edges.

Perimeter of semicircle

$\frac{1}{2} \times \pi d = \frac{1}{2} \times \pi \times 1$

$= \frac{\pi}{2}$ ✓

Annotating your diagram is very useful. It shows what you have found and what you need to find. To find the unknown lengths, consider the line markings that show which lines are of equal length.

Total perimeter:

$= 1 + 0.5 + 1.25 + 1.5 + 2 + 1.75 + 0.5 + 0.5 + 1 + \frac{\pi}{2} + 2$

$= 13.57079...$ ✓

$= 14\,m$ *(rounded up to nearest m)* ✓

When the perimeter has multiple sections, use a methodical approach to make sure you don't miss any out. In this example, it starts at the bottom left vertex and works around each edge, going anti-clockwise.

Having taped the edges, Sabiha applies two coats of paint as a base layer. 150 ml of paint will cover 1 square metre.

b) How many litres of paint will Sabiha need for her base layers? Give your answer to 2 significant figures. *(7 marks)*

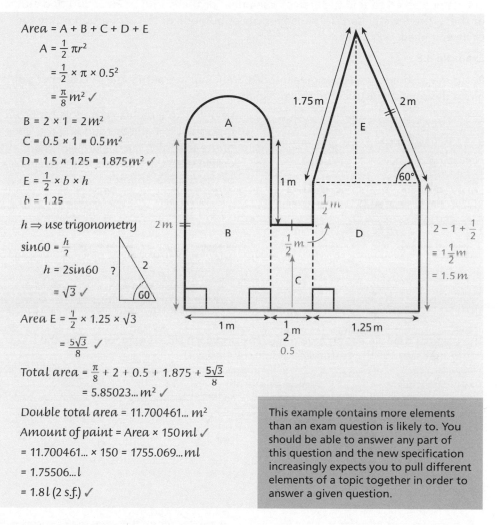

Area = A + B + C + D + E

$A = \frac{1}{2}\pi r^2$

$\quad = \frac{1}{2} \times \pi \times 0.5^2$

$\quad = \frac{\pi}{8} m^2$ ✓

$B = 2 \times 1 = 2 m^2$

$C = 0.5 \times 1 = 0.5 m^2$

$D = 1.5 \times 1.25 = 1.875 m^2$ ✓

$E = \frac{1}{2} \times b \times h$

$b = 1.25$

$h \Rightarrow$ use trigonometry

$\sin 60 = \frac{h}{2}$

$\quad h = 2\sin 60$

$\quad = \sqrt{3}$ ✓

Area E $= \frac{1}{2} \times 1.25 \times \sqrt{3}$

$\quad = \frac{5\sqrt{3}}{8}$ ✓

Total area $= \frac{\pi}{8} + 2 + 0.5 + 1.875 + \frac{5\sqrt{3}}{8}$

$\quad = 5.85023... m^2$ ✓

Double total area $= 11.700461... m^2$

Amount of paint = Area $\times$ 150ml ✓

$= 11.700461... \times 150 = 1755.069... ml$

$= 1.75506... l$

$= 1.8 l$ (2 s.f.) ✓

This example contains more elements than an exam question is likely to. You should be able to answer any part of this question and the new specification increasingly expects you to pull different elements of a topic together in order to answer a given question.

6.8 Area of a Sector

You can be asked to find the area of a segment or the length of an arc. To find either of these, use the standard formulae for circles but look at the proportion of the full circle you need.

Example 6.8

Rufus makes brooches. His original brooch is an equilateral triangle. A customer sends him a design with instructions shown below.

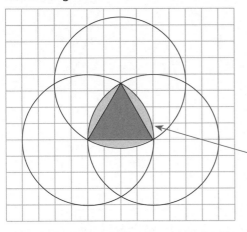

I would like a reuleaux triangle brooch making. It is made by rounding the sides of the triangle. The circles have been drawn with their centres at the vertices of the original triangle.

The distance between the vertices should be the same as the original triangle brooch.

Reuleaux triangles are shapes of constant width, which means that they will roll evenly. The most common example of a shape of constant width is the 50p piece.

The original triangle has an area of $4\sqrt{3}$ cm^2 and each side is 4 cm long. Find the additional area for the customer's design. *(4 marks)*

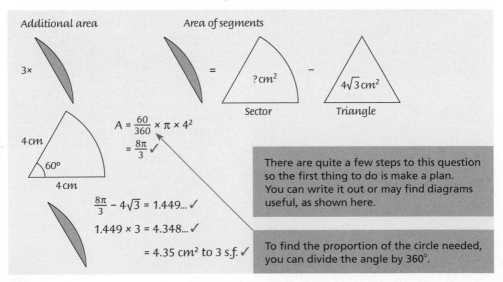

Additional area

Area of segments

$3\times$

$=$

? cm^2

$-$

$4\sqrt{3}$ cm^2

Sector

Triangle

4 cm

$60°$

4 cm

$A = \dfrac{60}{360} \times \pi \times 4^2$

$= \dfrac{8\pi}{3}$ ✓

$\dfrac{8\pi}{3} - 4\sqrt{3} = 1.449...$ ✓

$1.449 \times 3 = 4.348...$ ✓

$= 4.35$ cm^2 to 3 s.f. ✓

There are quite a few steps to this question so the first thing to do is make a plan. You can write it out or may find diagrams useful, as shown here.

To find the proportion of the circle needed, you can divide the angle by 360°.

6.9 Plans, Elevations and Projections

Plans, elevations and projections are used by architects, engineers and builders to communicate their ideas. Being able to understand and visualise shapes from plans and elevations is a very useful skill.

Example 6.9

Alison is designing a new office block. Below are the plan and two elevation drawings of her design.

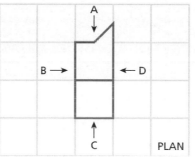

PLAN

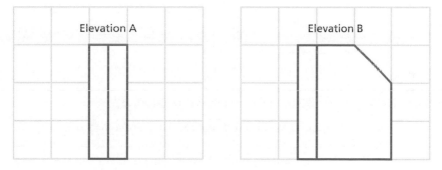

a) In the space provided, complete the remaining elevations. *(4 marks)*

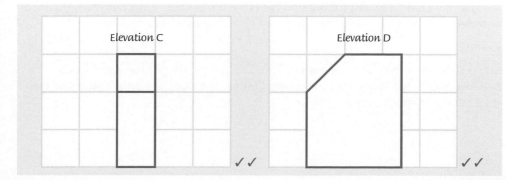

b) In the space below, draw a projection of the building. *(2 marks)*

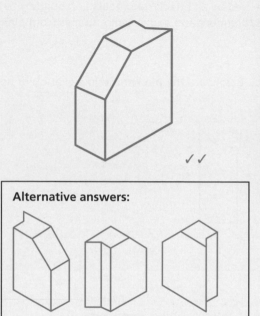

To draw your projection, choose a corner to start from. This is one of four possible projections, looking from corner CD. Make sure the lines that are meant to be parallel are parallel, e.g. the flat roof and the ground. Don't worry if the proportions aren't quite how you want them. The main thing is that you are able to represent the shape. Don't waste too much time on small details.

Alternative answers:

6.10 Bearings, Measurement and Scales

Bearings are used to communicate about direction. They are a measure of turn (number of degrees) and are taken from the North. Generally a bearing is given from point A to point B, or of point B from point A. Make sure you start at the correct one.

You might be asked to create a construction or use given bearings to find an answer using angle facts. Look out for parallel lines (the north lines). Questions can require a geometric approach to solve them but may also include scales and ratios.

Example 6.10

Mia is flying her plane at a constant height. She passes over Bilston and takes a bearing of 060° for 10 km until she is over Chirley. She then flies on a bearing of 146° for 11 km to reach Deeston.

Using a suitable scale, construct a diagram to represent Mia's flight and use it to estimate the bearing and horizontal distance she would take in order to be back above Bilston. *(6 marks)*

'Suitable scale'

1 cm = 2 km ✓

A suitable scale is one that is as large as possible for the space (to minimise the effect of residual errors) but is also one that is easy to work with. Consider starting with a little sketch so you can decide where in the space you should start.

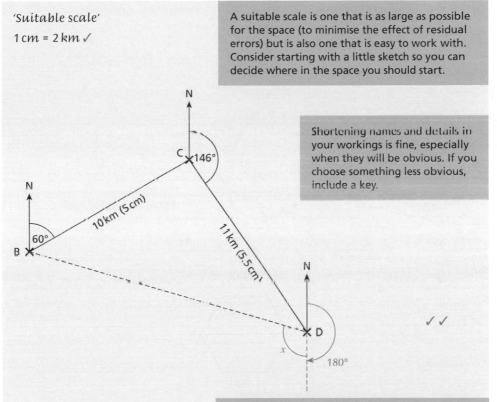

Shortening names and details in your workings is fine, especially when they will be obvious. If you choose something less obvious, include a key.

$x \approx 105°$ (based on measurement to the nearest degree)

Bearing of B from D ≈ 285° ✓ ✓

BD ≈ 7.7 cm

BD ≈ 7.7 × 2 ≈ 15.4 km ✓

When constructing, a certain level of error is expected as measurements can only be performed to a certain accuracy. The accurate answer is 285.5…° and the length is 15.37356…km but it is impossible to achieve this accuracy without calculation. Your answer must be right for your diagram and full marks will be gained if all aspects of your diagram fall within the allowed level of accuracy (generally within a few degrees).

6.11 Surface Area, Volume and Use of Formulae

Compound volumes are ones that you can split into recognisable shapes in order to calculate the total volume. It might be that you need to remove a section or add sections together, but spotting the parts is key in solving these questions.

Example 6.11

A children's puzzle is made up of three prisms: a cylinder, a flower and an equilateral triangular prism. Each prism is 1.5 cm deep.

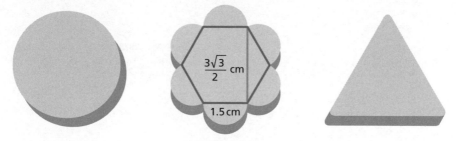

The flower is a regular hexagon, with edge length 1.5 cm.
From each edge, a semicircle forms the petals.
This diagram shows the hexagon in the middle of the flower.

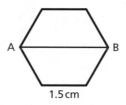

a) What is the length of AB? Explain your answer. *(2 marks)*

AB = 3 cm ✓

Since a regular hexagon is made up of
six equilateral triangles, as shown.
All the lengths are equal so AB is twice
the length of the given edge. ✓

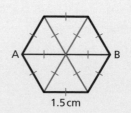

b) What is the volume of the flower prism? Give your answer to 3 significant figures.
(8 marks)

Volume of a prism is:
Area of the face × Length

Area of face = Area of hexagon +
Area of 6 semicircles (3 full circles) ✓

There are many ways to treat the composite shape. You could split it into two equal trapezia by joining opposite vertices. If you know the area of a trapezium, then this might be a good option.

Area of semicircles:

Each circle: $A = \pi r^2 = \pi\left(\frac{3}{4}\right)^2 = \frac{9\pi}{16}$ ✓

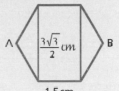

All semicircles = $3 \times \frac{9\pi}{16} = \frac{27\pi}{16}$

Area of hexagon = Area of rectangle + Area of 2 triangles

Area of rectangle = $\frac{3\sqrt{3}}{2} \times 1.5 = \frac{9\sqrt{3}}{4}$ ✓

Area of both triangles = $2 \times \frac{1}{2} \times b \times h$

$$h = \frac{3 - 1.5}{2} = 0.75 ✓$$

If you cannot find the area, even after having a good go at it, it can be worth giving the area a number (a good guess) and then using that to get the method marks for the rest of the question.

Area of triangles = $0.75 \times \frac{3\sqrt{3}}{2} = \frac{9\sqrt{3}}{8}$ ✓

Total area of hexagon = $\frac{9\sqrt{3}}{4} + \frac{9\sqrt{3}}{8} = \frac{27\sqrt{3}}{8}$ ✓

Total area = $\frac{27\sqrt{3}}{8} + \frac{27\pi}{16} = 11.147109...$ cm^2

Volume = $11.1471... \times 1.5$ ✓

$= 16.7206636...$

$= 16.7$ cm^3 (3 s.f.) ✓

Most calculators will give answers in surd form (with a square root sign in it). It is good to keep your working in surd form as it is accurate. You can also use the memory function on your calculator to store these numbers and save time when you need to use them again. Get to know your calculator and ask to be shown the memory function if you don't already know how to use it.

As the question asks for '3 significant figures', you need to convert into a decimal for the final answer.

c) What is the surface area of the cylinder given it has a diameter of 3 cm? *(4 marks)*

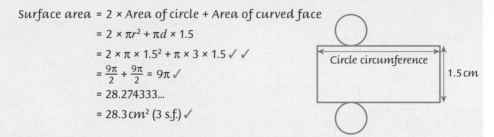

Surface area = 2 × Area of circle + Area of curved face

$= 2 \times \pi r^2 + \pi d \times 1.5$

$= 2 \times \pi \times 1.5^2 + \pi \times 3 \times 1.5$ ✓✓

$= \frac{9\pi}{2} + \frac{9\pi}{2} = 9\pi$ ✓

$= 28.274333...$

$= 28.3 \, cm^2$ (3 s.f.) ✓

6.12 Known Trigonometric Ratios

You need to know the trigonometric ratios (the value of $\sin\theta$, $\cos\theta$ and $\tan\theta$) for $\theta = 0°$, 30°, 45°, 60° and 90°. The ratio tells you the relationship between two of the sides in a right-angled triangle.

Example 6.12 📱

A mast, of height h m, is held in a vertical position by three ropes, which are attached to the horizontal ground near the base of the mast.
Ropes A and B meet the ground at angles of $\theta°$ and $2\theta°$ respectively.

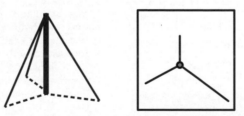

a) In terms of h and θ, find expressions for the length of rope A and rope B. *(2 marks)*

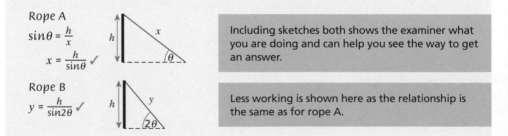

Rope A

$\sin\theta = \frac{h}{x}$

$x = \frac{h}{\sin\theta}$ ✓

Including sketches both shows the examiner what you are doing and can help you see the way to get an answer.

Rope B

$y = \frac{h}{\sin2\theta}$ ✓

Less working is shown here as the relationship is the same as for rope A.

The mast is 6 m high and the longest rope is 12 m long.
Rope C meets the ground h m from the base of the mast.

b) Find the lengths of the other two ropes, giving your answers in exact form. *(3 marks)*

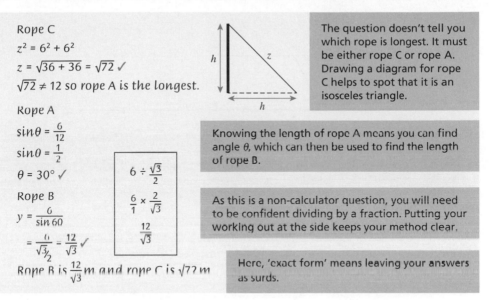

Rope C

$z^2 = 6^2 + 6^2$

$z = \sqrt{36 + 36} = \sqrt{72}$ ✓

$\sqrt{72} \neq 12$ so rope A is the longest.

The question doesn't tell you which rope is longest. It must be either rope C or rope A. Drawing a diagram for rope C helps to spot that it is an isosceles triangle.

Rope A

$\sin\theta = \frac{6}{12}$

$\sin\theta = \frac{1}{2}$

$\theta = 30°$ ✓

Knowing the length of rope A means you can find angle θ, which can then be used to find the length of rope B.

$6 \div \frac{\sqrt{3}}{2}$

$\frac{6}{1} \times \frac{2}{\sqrt{3}}$

$\frac{12}{\sqrt{3}}$

Rope B

$y = \frac{6}{\sin 60}$

$= \frac{6}{\frac{\sqrt{3}}{2}} = \frac{12}{\sqrt{3}}$ ✓

As this is a non-calculator question, you will need to be confident dividing by a fraction. Putting your working out at the side keeps your method clear.

Rope B is $\frac{12}{\sqrt{3}}$ m and rope C is $\sqrt{72}$ m

Here, 'exact form' means leaving your answers as surds.

6.13 Vectors – Diagrams, Arguments and Proof

Vectors are used to represent things that have both magnitude and direction. They can be represented by a directed line; the magnitude is represented by the length of the line and the arrow shows the direction.

Vectors can be drawn, referred to as column vectors, given names (lowercase letters underlined when handwritten; but shown in bold when in print) and manipulated algebraically.

Example 6.13

Vector $\overrightarrow{AB}$ = **a** and vector $\overrightarrow{BC}$ = **b**

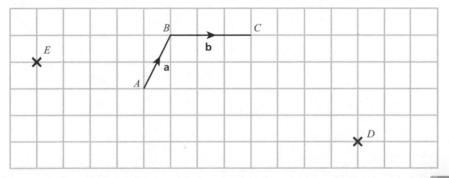

a) Find an expression in terms of **a** and **b** to describe $\overrightarrow{AD}$. *(1 mark)*

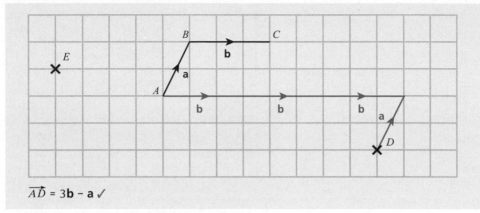

$\overrightarrow{AD}$ = 3**b** − **a** ✓

b) Find an expression in terms of **a** and **b** to describe $\overrightarrow{DE}$. *(2 marks)*

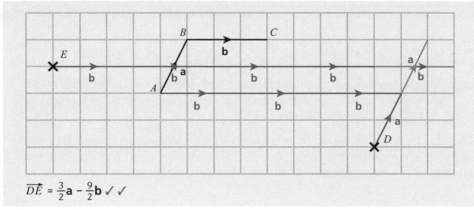

$\overrightarrow{DE}$ = $\frac{3}{2}$**a** − $\frac{9}{2}$**b** ✓ ✓

For more on the topics covered in this chapter, see pages 22–25, 46–51, 58–63, 82–87 & 106–109 of the Collins Edexcel Maths Foundation Revision Guide.

Geometry and Measures: Key Notes

- You need to know the names and properties of polygons (up to 10 sides) and circles. For triangles and quadrilaterals, you need to know the properties (angles, parallel lines, etc.) and the names (isosceles, kite, equilateral, trapezium, etc.). Make sure you know how to spell them correctly.
- A regular polygon has all edges (and all angles) equal.
- When constructing, leave in your construction marks. If there aren't any, you might not get the marks. Practise working with your pair of compasses for accuracy.
- When working with angle reasoning, you need to <u>justify</u> each stage of your working. Even if your numerical answer is right, you won't get marks unless you can justify and explain your steps.
- There is a lot of assumed knowledge for this topic, e.g. angle rules, trigonometric values and formulae for areas, perimeters and circumferences. See Chapter 2 for ideas of how to help learn rules and formulae; see Chapter 10 for what formulae are given and those you need to learn.
- Geometry can get context heavy. Try to see the maths the examiners are testing you on and don't get too hung up on the context. If you need to make assumptions, state them clearly.
- To describe a transformation fully:
  - Translation: give the column vector
  - Reflection: give the line of reflection, e.g. $x = 2$, $y = -4$, $y = x$, etc.
  - Rotation: give the **centre of rotation**, e.g. (2, −2); the amount of turn, e.g. through 90°; and the direction of turn, e.g. clockwise
  - Enlargement: give the **centre of enlargement**, e.g. (0, 3), and the scale factor, e.g. 0.5.
- Enlargements can also have a fractional scale factor which, if the fraction is between 0 and 1, would mean that the image (new shape created) would get smaller in relation to the original shape.
- If a question involves a right-angled triangle, consider:
  - Pythagoras' theorem if you have two sides and need to find the third side
  - **Trigonometry** (SOH CAH TOA) if you have two sides and want to find an angle or have an angle (as well as the right angle) and a side but want to find another side. The trigonometric functions tell you what the ratio between two particular sides is in a set of similar triangles.
- If you are stuck, or not sure what the question is asking for, think about what you can do. If there is a rectangle in the diagram, you can find the area, perimeter, diagonals, etc.
- Vectors are quantities with both direction and magnitude (size). They can be expressed as column vectors, e.g. $\begin{pmatrix} 4 \\ -2 \end{pmatrix}$ which means 4 right and −2 up (or 2 down).
- To write a vector in algebraic terms, underline the vector values (in printed text they are shown in bold).

7 Probability

Probability is used to look at the chance, or likelihood, of an event happening. It is useful in a variety of ways, from game theory to genetics. You will need to have a good understanding of working with decimals, fractions and percentages to tackle this topic successfully. Questions tend to be given in a context, a 'real life' problem to solve, and can get quite wordy, so take your time and explain clearly what you are doing at each stage.

7.1 Counters in a Bag

The classic example is of randomly selecting coloured counters (sweets, marbles, coins, etc.) from a bag (pot, jar, etc.). The theoretical probability of an outcome (for example blue) can be found by considering the number of blue counters and dividing it by how many counters there are altogether. This is a base for many questions.

Example 7.1 📱

There are three different colours of counter in a bag. There are 4 purple counters, 6 orange counters and 5 yellow counters. Maya takes a counter randomly from the bag.

a) What is the probability that Maya gets a purple counter? *(1 mark)*

There are $4 + 6 + 5 = 15$ *counters in the bag altogether.*

$P(purple) = \frac{4}{15}$ ✓

Probability is:

$$\frac{\text{Number of favourable outcomes}}{\text{Total number of possible outcomes}}$$

b) What is the probability that she will get a blue counter? *(1 mark)*

$P(blue) = 0$ ✓

As there are no blue counters in the bag, it is impossible that she will pick a blue counter. You could also say the probability is:

$$\frac{\text{Number of favourable outcomes}}{\text{Total number of possible outcomes}} = \frac{0}{15}$$

c) Maya replaces her counter and adds more purple counters to the bag until the probability of getting purple is $\frac{1}{2}$.

How many purple counters does she add? *(3 marks)*

$6 + 5 = 11$ ✓ $11 - 4 = 7$ ✓ *Maya adds 7 more purple counters.* ✓	There are many ways to model this. Choose a way that you understand. The main step in this question is recognising that if the probability is $\frac{1}{2}$ then there must be the same number of purple counters as there are of orange and yellow combined. 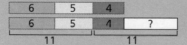

7.2 Frequency Trees

A **frequency tree** shows the numbers involved in a combined event. If there are only two parts, then a two-way table can also be used (unless the question specifies that you should use a frequency tree).

Example 7.2 📖

150 volunteers took part in a trial of a new headache cure. They were either given the drug or a placebo. The participants were then asked after 30 minutes, then again after 1 hour, if they felt an improvement. All those who felt an improvement after 30 minutes still felt an improvement after 1 hour.

The following frequency tree shows the results.

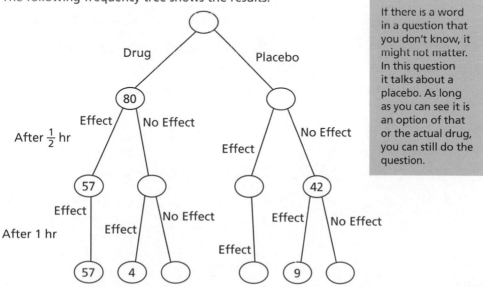

> If there is a word in a question that you don't know, it might not matter. In this question it talks about a placebo. As long as you can see it is an option of that or the actual drug, you can still do the question.

a) Complete the frequency tree. *(2 marks)*

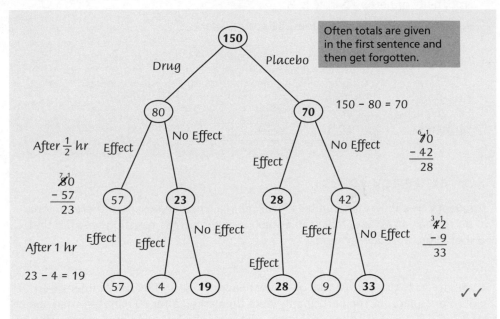

b) What is the probability that a person chosen at random was given the placebo? *(1 mark)*

$$P(placebo) = \frac{70}{150} = \frac{7}{15} \checkmark$$

c) What is the probability that a person selected at random felt no effect even after 1 hour? *(2 marks)*

$$P(no\ effect) = \frac{19 + 33}{150} \checkmark = \frac{52}{150} = \frac{26}{75} \checkmark$$

7.3 Experimental Probability

When you flip a fair coin, each outcome – heads (H) or tails (T) – is equally likely. This is true every time you flip the coin, whatever the last result was. This means that the result HTHT, in that order, is just as likely as TTHT or HHHH.

If a sample or experiment doesn't have many results, it is unlikely to represent the theoretical probability (in this case 0.5). If you increase the number of results, then the experimental probability becomes a better representation of the theoretical probability.

Example 7.3 📧

Jermaine is rolling a dice and gets the following results:

Score	1	2	3	4	5	6
Frequency	2	3	6	1	2	1

a) Jermaine says the dice is biased. Is he correct? Justify your answer. *(1 mark)*

Jermaine may be correct but he doesn't have enough evidence to support his conclusion at this time. There are relatively few results in this experiment. To be able to judge if the dice is biased, the experiment would need to be repeated many more times. ✓

Being asked to justify your answer means that you need to support your answer with good mathematical steps. A paragraph isn't necessary but some words can help to explain what you are doing.

Jermaine rolls a different dice until he has rolled it 500 times. His results table looks like this:

Score	1	2	3	4	5	6
Frequency	80	87	79	86	83	85

b) Jermaine says that this is a fair dice. Is he correct? Justify your answer. *(1 mark)*

Jermaine is correct. All the frequencies are approximately the same. ✓

It isn't likely that all the frequencies will be exactly the same – what matters is that they are approximately the same.

7.4 Exhaustive/Complementary Outcomes and Predicting Results

Many questions boil down to the outcome of an event being one result (A) or not being that result (not A). For example, when flipping a coin the outcome could be 'heads' or 'not heads' (tails). When you add the probabilities of all the complementary outcomes, the result is 1 (it is certain that the result will either be A or not be A). P(A) + P(not A) = 1

You can predict results using probability by multiplying the number of trials by the probability of the required outcome.

Example 7.4 📱

A set of cards have A, B, C or D written on them. A game is played by randomly picking a card, then replacing it in the pack.

The table shows the probability of picking a card with A, B or D on it.

Card	A	B	C	D
Probability	0.43	0.2		0.09

Often these questions might have a part **a)** to find the missing probability and a part **b)** to use an existing probability to predict. It is important that you can plan out the steps when answering these questions yourself.

Edward is going to model playing the game 75 times. Approximately how many times should he expect to get a C? *(4 marks)*

P(not C) = 0.43 + 0.2 + 0.09 = 0.72 ✓
P(C) = 1 − P(not C) = 1 − 0.72 = 0.28 ✓
0.28 × 75 = 21 ✓

Edward would expect to get a C
approximately 21 times. ✓

$$\begin{array}{r} 0.43 \\ 0.20 \\ + \ 0.09 \\ \hline 0.72 \end{array}$$

$$\begin{array}{r} 1.\overset{9}{\cancel{0}}0 \\ - \ 0.72 \\ \hline 0.28 \end{array}$$

Marks are often lost on relatively simple calculations – written methods can help to reduce this risk. Take your time and show your working.

7.5 Experimental Probability and Predictions

The more results in an experiment or items in a sample, the closer the experimental probability gets to representing the theoretical probability. Theoretical probabilities are obtained from knowing enough information but in some situations it is impossible to know all the information.

Example 7.5

Clare places 15 counters into a bag without looking at the colours. The counters could be red, yellow or blue. She picks a counter randomly, notes its colour and then replaces it.

After 15 goes, Clare's results table looks like this:

Colour	Red	Yellow	Blue
Frequency	0	9	6

a) Clare says there must be more yellow counters than blue and that there cannot be any red counters in the bag. Is she correct? *(1 mark)*

> *Clare might be correct but she doesn't have enough information to support this idea.* ✓

Clare repeats the experiment many more times.

Colour	Red	Yellow	Blue
Frequency	16	166	118

b) Calculate the experimental probability of getting each colour based on her results. *(3 marks)*

> *Total number* = 16 + 166 + 118
>
> $\qquad$ = 300
>
> *Experimental probability of getting red* = $\frac{16}{300}$ = $\frac{4}{75}$ ✓
>
> *Experimental probability of getting yellow* = $\frac{166}{300}$ = $\frac{83}{150}$ ✓
>
> *Experimental probability of getting blue* = $\frac{118}{300}$ = $\frac{59}{150}$ ✓

c) How many of each colour counter would you predict there are in the bag? *(3 marks)*

> *Number of red counters* ≈ $\frac{4}{75}$ × 15 ≈ 0.8 ≈ 1 ✓
>
> *Number of yellow counters* ≈ $\frac{83}{150}$ × 15 ≈ 8.3 ≈ 8 ✓
>
> *Number of blue counters* ≈ $\frac{59}{150}$ × 15 ≈ 5.9 ≈ 6 ✓
>
> *I would predict that there are 1 red counter, 8 yellow counters and 6 blue counters in the bag.*

7.6 Sets and Combinations

When considering probabilities, it is useful to be able to find the different possible outcomes to an event. This could be the different combinations of scores on two dice or different combinations of sandwich fillings. You need to be systematic in your approach when asked to list all the possible combinations. Sample space diagrams could be an option, especially if there are only two things being chosen and if you need to combine the results in some way (such as by adding the scores).

Example 7.6

Lunch bags are made up in a school and contain a sandwich, a drink and a piece of fruit.

As a sandwich, pupils can have either cheese, egg or ham. The drink can be either water or orange juice. The fruit is either a banana or an apple.

a) Write down all the possible combinations that could be in the lunch bags. *(2 marks)*

Key: C = cheese, E = egg, H = ham, W = water, O = orange juice, B = banana, A = apple

Combinations:

CWA	EWA	HWA
CWB	EWB	HWB
COA	EOA	HOA
COB	EOB	HOB ✓✓

By organising the answer into columns and filling in the options systematically, you are less likely to forget to include something. In this case you could either work down each column, finding the options to go with each sandwich choice, or you could work along the rows.

b) There is one of each combination left on the counter. They get muddled up and one is selected at random.

What is the probability that it contains water and an apple? *(2 marks)*

CWA	EWA	HWA ✓
CWB	EWB	HWB
COA	EOA	HOA
COB	EOB	HOB

$P(WA) = \frac{3}{12} = \frac{1}{4}$ ✓

c) Fiona doesn't eat ham. She chooses a bag but replaces it until she gets one without ham.

What is the probability that she will get a cheese sandwich with orange juice? *(3 marks)*

CWA	EWA	HWA
CWB	EWB	HWB
COA	EOA	HOA ✓
COB ✓	EOB	HOB

As Fiona replaces any bag with a ham sandwich, you can ignore the ham column.

$P(CO) = \frac{2}{8} = \frac{1}{4}$ ✓

7.7 Two-way Tables and Probability

Two-way tables are a great way to represent situations where there are two lots of information. Sometimes you will be able to choose how you work out the answer but at other times the question will specify a method, so you need to be good at all the methods and know when to use them.

Example 7.7

A youth group is planning a film night for 76 people. The organisers plan to have three rooms with different films showing: rom-com, adventure and sci-fi. Each person attending will have either pizza or popcorn to eat. 34 people say they will watch the sci-fi film. 12 people want to watch the rom-com.

The organisers have bought 7 pizzas, each of which will be cut into quarters. If each person who requested pizza has a quarter, there will be one piece spare. There is an equal number of pizza eaters watching each film.

a) What is the probability that a person chosen at random wants to watch an adventure film? *(3 marks)*

Pizza pieces:
$7 \times 4 - 1 = 27$;
$27 \div 3 = 9$
∴ 9 pizza eaters in each room.

	Rom-com	Adventure	Sci-fi	Total	
Pizza	9	9	9	27	✓
Popcorn	3	21	25	49	
Total	12	30	34	76	✓

$P(adventure) = \frac{30}{76} = \frac{15}{38}$ ✓

b) What is the probability that a person chosen randomly from the rom-com room is going to be eating popcorn? *(2 marks)*

In the rom-com room there are 12 people.

3 are eating popcorn. ✓

$\frac{3}{12} = \frac{1}{4}$ ✓

7.8 Sample Space Diagrams

A sample space diagram shows all the possible outcomes of an event or combination of events. Within each event, all possible outcomes must be equally likely. This is often used for combined events such as rolling a fair dice and spinning a fair spinner.

Example 7.8

At a school fair, Roisin sets up a game in which a player spins the two spinners shown. They add together the two numbers obtained to get a final score.

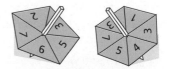

Roisin will give a prize of £2.50 for a winning final score but she does not know what score she should use.

a) Which final score should Roisin use in order to maximise her profits? *(3 marks)*

	2	3	5	6	7
1	3	4	6	7	8
3	5	6	8	9	10
3	5	6	8	9	10
4	6	7	9	10	11
5	7	8	10	11	12
7	9	10	12	13	14	✓✓

Each edge of the spinner is equally likely, so you can set up a sample space diagram to show all the different (equally likely) outcomes. NB: there are two number 3s on the hexagonal spinner, so they both need to be included.

Roisin could use any of the numbers that just appear once as they have the same probability of being chosen.

3, 4, 13 or 14 ✓

Any one of these answers would gain the final answer mark.

b) 120 people will play the game during the fair. If Roisin charges 20p a go, how much profit can she expect to make? *(3 marks)*

> If this is on the non-calculator paper, take your time and show your written method of calculation where relevant.

Total income = 0.20 × 120 = £24 ✓

Number of prizes expected = 120 × $\frac{1}{30}$ = 4

Predicted prize money handed out
= 2.50 × 4 = £10 ✓

Profit = 24 − 10 = £14.00 ✓

> The probability of getting a winning score is $\frac{1}{30}$ as there are 5 × 6 possible equally likely results, of which only one is 'favourable'.

> Show clearly what each calculation finds to make it easy for you to follow your own working. It will also help for checking and for the examiner to mark it.

7.9 Venn Diagrams

A Venn diagram is good for dealing with options that are not **mutually exclusive**, i.e. things that can both be true at the same time. These are represented by the overlap sections in the diagram.

Example 7.9

A group of 32 students were asked if they like to watch football or rugby.

- 8 students didn't like to watch either football or rugby.
- 19 students said they enjoyed watching football.
- 12 students said that they enjoyed watching rugby.

Use this information to draw a Venn diagram and find the probability that a student chosen at random likes to watch both football and rugby. *(3 marks)*

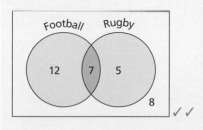

P(student likes both) = $\frac{7}{32}$ ✓

> There are two options and a neither. You can set up a Venn diagram with two circles to represent football and rugby.

> As 8 students don't like either, there are 24 students who like either football, rugby or both.

> You can find how many like both by adding together those that like football (19) and those that like rugby (12) and taking away 24. This finds the number that must be in the overlap section.

> Having found the overlap, you can fill in all the remaining sections. Check all the relevant sections are right by considering how many are in each circle and that altogether there are 32.

7.10 Probability Trees

Probability trees are useful for dependent events, i.e. where the outcome of one event affects the probability of the second. They may involve 'non-replacement', for example where:

- a sweet is taken from a jar and eaten, then a second one is taken
- the probability of snow on a particular day changes if it snowed the day before.

Probability trees run horizontally and have the probability written on the branches with the outcome at the end of each branch. As you go, check that the sum of all probabilities on a set of branches coming from the same point is 1. Probabilities can be written as fractions, decimals or percentages but, as this involves multiplication, fractions are often easiest if you get a choice.

Example 7.10

The probability that Tegwen has a bath on a Saturday is 0.68. If she has a bath on Saturday, the probability that she will have a bath on Sunday is 0.35. If she doesn't have a bath on Saturday, the probability that she will have a bath on Sunday is 0.82.

a) What is the probability that Tegwen will have two baths this weekend? *(4 marks)*

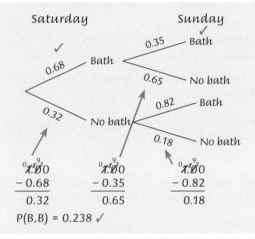

Multiply along the branches.

P(B,B) = 0.68 × 0.35 = 0.238 ✓

P(B,N) = 0.68 × 0.65 = 0.442

P(N,B) = 0.32 × 0.82 = 0.2624

P(N,N) = 0.32 × 0.18 = 0.0576

As the question was given in decimals, it is best to give your answer in decimals.

$$\begin{array}{ccc} {}^{0}\cancel{1}.\cancel{0}0 & {}^{0}\cancel{1}.\cancel{0}0 & {}^{0}\cancel{1}.\cancel{0}0 \\ -\,0.68 & -\,0.35 & -\,0.82 \\ \hline 0.32 & 0.65 & 0.18 \end{array}$$

P(B,B) = 0.238 ✓

b) What is the probability that Tegwen will have at least one bath this weekend? *(3 marks)*

P(B,B) + P(B,N) + P(N,B) = 0.238 + 0.442 + 0.2624 ✓ ✓

= 0.9424 ✓

7.11 Combined Events, Dependence and Tree Diagrams

When considering more than one event, you need to consider the effect of one on the other. Sometimes the first event has no effect on the second, but if there is dependence, the outcome of one event changes the probabilities of the second event. A **tree diagram** can be useful to clearly show what is happening.

Example 7.11

A bakery sells trays of cupcakes with different flavoured fillings. Laura orders a tray with 7 lemon flavoured centres, 4 chocolate centres and 1 salted caramel centre. She takes a cupcake at random and eats it. She then takes a second cupcake.

a) What is the probability that Laura got two of her favourite lemon flavoured cupcakes? *(4 marks)*

The question doesn't specify what method to use. As there is a change in probability between the first and second event – a 'non-replacement' question – a probability tree is a good way to represent the situation.

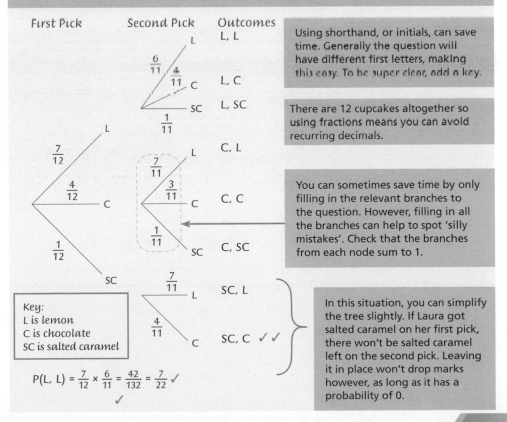

Using shorthand, or initials, can save time. Generally the question will have different first letters, making this easy. To be super clear, add a key.

There are 12 cupcakes altogether so using fractions means you can avoid recurring decimals.

You can sometimes save time by only filling in the relevant branches to the question. However, filling in all the branches can help to spot 'silly mistakes'. Check that the branches from each node sum to 1.

In this situation, you can simplify the tree slightly. If Laura got salted caramel on her first pick, there won't be salted caramel left on the second pick. Leaving it in place won't drop marks however, as long as it has a probability of 0.

Key:
L is lemon
C is chocolate
SC is salted caramel

$$P(L, L) = \frac{7}{12} \times \frac{6}{11} = \frac{42}{132} = \frac{7}{22} \checkmark$$

b) What is the probability that Laura got two cupcakes that were different flavours?
(4 marks)

First Pick	Second Pick	Outcomes	

$P(L, C) = \frac{7}{12} \times \frac{4}{11} = \frac{28}{132}$

$P(L, SC) = \frac{7}{12} \times \frac{1}{11} = \frac{7}{132}$ ✓

$P(C, L) = \frac{4}{12} \times \frac{7}{11} = \frac{28}{132}$

$P(C, SC) = \frac{4}{12} \times \frac{1}{11} = \frac{4}{132}$ ✓

$P(SC, L) = \frac{1}{12} \times \frac{7}{11} = \frac{7}{132}$

$P(SC, C) = \frac{1}{12} \times \frac{4}{11} = \frac{4}{132}$ ✓

Highlight the required branches on the tree diagram.

Don't simplify at this stage, even if you can, as your next step is to add the different combinations. In this case, as in most cases, the denominator will be the same along each branch, making the fraction sum easier.

$P(different\ flavours) = \frac{28}{132} + \frac{7}{132} + \frac{28}{132} + \frac{4}{132} + \frac{7}{132} + \frac{4}{132}$

$= \frac{78}{132} = \frac{13}{22}$ ✓

The correct answer could also be found by:
$1 - P$ (two the same flavour) =
$1 - (\frac{7}{22} + \frac{2}{22} + 0) = \frac{13}{22}$

7.12 Approaching Questions From Different Angles

Examiners will always search for new ways of approaching questions to check that you understand the subject material. Think about how you might approach similar questions.

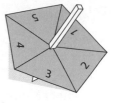

Example 7.12

A spinner is numbered 1 to 5.
John spins the spinner until he gets a 4.

Work out the probability that John spins the spinner:

a) exactly once. *(1 mark)*

Assume the spinner/dice/coin is fair unless the question says otherwise.

$P(4 \text{ on first spin}) = \frac{1}{5}$ ✓

The probability that John spins the spinner once is the probability that he gets a 4 on his first spin. There is one 4 and five possibilities so the probability is one out of five.

b) exactly twice. *(2 marks)*

You might want to use a diagram to help you model what is going on. Here is a tree diagram showing the possible outcomes. Consider further parts to the question when setting up your diagram; you might be able to save yourself some time later.

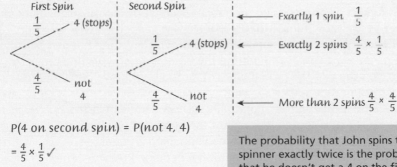

$P(4 \text{ on second spin}) = P(\text{not } 4, 4)$

$= \frac{4}{5} \times \frac{1}{5}$ ✓

$= \frac{4}{25}$ ✓

The probability that John spins the spinner exactly twice is the probability that he doesn't get a 4 on the first spin, then does on the second.

c) more than twice. *(2 marks)*

$P(\text{more than 2 spins}) = 1 - P(\text{1st}) - P(\text{2nd})$

$= 1 - \frac{1}{5} - \frac{4}{25} = 1 - \frac{9}{25}$ ✓

$= \frac{16}{25}$ ✓

The probability that he spins the spinner more than twice is the probability that he didn't just spin it once or twice.

Having a second method can help you check answers. Also, if you are stuck, trying a different method might help. In this case, looking at the tree diagram would also give the same result.

For more on the topics covered in this chapter, see pages 32–35 of the Collins Edexcel Maths Foundation Revision Guide.

Probability: Key Notes

- Probability is used to measure, consider and communicate about chance and likelihood.
- The probability scale goes from 0 (impossible) to 1 (certain).

0   0.5   1

- If you find a negative probability or a probability greater than 1, you know there has been a mistake.
- Probabilities can be expressed as fractions, decimals or percentages. You should take your lead from the question wherever possible. <u>Do not</u> use ratios or 'out of'. If the question does not give you one, use whichever you are most comfortable with.
- There is a lot of specific terminology and notation – check the Glossary on page 139.
- The theoretical probability of any particular outcome to an event is $\frac{\text{The number of possible favourable outcomes}}{\text{The total number of outcomes}}$, where each outcome is equally likely.
  - A favourable outcome is the outcome that you are calculating the probability for.
- An experiment or a sample should be large enough so that the probabilities and proportions of the sample (or generated in the experiment) can be used to estimate the proportions and probabilities of the whole group (the theoretical probabilities).
- You can predict outcomes using probability by multiplying the probability of the outcome by the total number of times the event happens.
- Mutually exclusive outcomes are outcomes that cannot both happen at the same time, e.g. getting a vowel and getting the letter G when selecting one letter at random. You can add the probabilities of mutually exclusive outcomes to find the probability of getting either of them.
- The sum of the probabilities of mutually exclusive and exhaustive outcomes to a given event is 1 (it is certain that one of the outcomes will happen).
- The probability of a particular outcome happening is equal to (1 – the probability of that outcome not happening). P(A) = 1 – P(not A)
- There are lots of diagrams you can use. Be careful to use the right one if it is stated in the question (especially note the difference between a frequency tree and a probability tree):
  - A sample space shows all the possible outcomes of an event. It can be used for a combination of two events but tends to get complicated beyond that.
  - Lists, tables, grids and trees can be used to represent combined events.
  - Frequency trees show the frequencies of particular outcomes at the ends of the branches. You read the frequencies and use them to find the probabilities.
  - Probability trees show the outcome at the end of each branch and the probability on the branch.

8 Statistics

Statistics is used widely to help understand situations. It involves collecting, analysing and representing data to provide greater understanding of situations. Almost every job will involve some sort of statistics, for example sports coaches look at performance data, doctors need to know about the effectiveness of treatments and businesses write reports for shareholders. It is often said that it is easy to lie with statistics and therefore it is very important to have a good understanding to avoid being misled.

8.1 Populations and Sampling

In statistics, the 'population' refers to everyone or everything that you are interested in. That could be all of the students at your school, all men aged 20 to 25 in the UK or it could refer to items such as all of the books in a library. If you want to find out information about a population, it is often unrealistic to use the whole population so a sample will be used.

Sampling Methods

A classic question is to be given a sampling method and asked whether it is a good one. It usually is not a good method, so you will need to explain the potential problems.

Example 8.1

Amy wants to research how many CDs people buy. She stands outside CD World on a Tuesday in December at 11am and asks every tenth person how many CDs they have bought this week. Evaluate this sampling method. *(2 marks)*

Amy's location means that many of the people she is asking will be customers of CD World and therefore likely to buy CDs regularly.

At 11am on a weekday, many people will be at work or school so her sample will not be representative.

In December, people could be buying Christmas presents, so their shopping habits may be different from a normal week.

By asking every tenth customer, she is taking a systematic sample and this means that the population should be evenly sampled. ✓✓

You are looking for any sources of bias. Try to think about parts of the population that may be missed out or over-represented.

There are two marks available so you will need to make two points. They must be sufficiently different so you cannot say some people will be at work and some people will be at school as these points are both highlighting a problem with the time of the study.

8.2 Measures of Location and Spread

There are times when it is useful to have summary statistics which give a quick, concise representation of the data. The three averages (**mean**, **median** and **mode**) and the **range** give information about the location of the data and how spread out it is. Often these measures are combined as part of a question about displaying data, but they can also be made into a harder question by requiring you to work backwards from information given. If the data has been grouped, additional steps are needed in order to find the averages from the table given.

Example 8.2.1 (finding unknowns)

There are eight children who have an average age of 14 years old. A pair of twins, Adam and Betty, join the group and the average age decreases to 13 years old. How old are Adam and Betty? *(3 marks)*

The total age of the
8 children is 8 × 14 = 112

When the twins join, the new
total is 10 × 13 = 130. ✓

The average takes the total and divides it by the number of values so you do the opposite here to find the total by multiplying the average by the number of children.

They are twins so must be the same age, which can be represented as x.

$2x + 112 = 130$ ✓

$2x = 18$

$x = 9$ so Adam and Betty
are 9 years old. ✓

You can set up an equation to solve with x as the twins' age.

Make sure the answer is obvious at the end.

The algebra makes it clear but you could choose to do this without it; just make sure you write down the steps you use.

Example 8.2.2 (averages from a table)

Mr Nyembo asks his form group how far they live from the school. The information is shown in the table.

Distance (d miles)	Frequency (f)
$0 < d \leqslant 1$	12
$1 < d \leqslant 2$	8
$2 < d \leqslant 5$	7
$5 < d \leqslant 10$	5

There are a number of different averages questions you can be asked from a table. You wouldn't usually get asked so many parts but this example shows some of the types of questions that might appear.

The data has been grouped into categories, which makes it easier to put into a table, but it loses some of its accuracy. It is no longer possible to know the exact distances the children live from the school, so the mode and the median will be given as a class and the mean will be an estimate.

a) Write down the modal class interval. *(1 mark)*

The modal class is $0 < d \leq 1$ miles. ✓ | The modal class is the category with the highest frequency. Make sure you state the category, not the frequency (as that is a common mistake).

b) Find the median class interval. *(2 marks)*

To find the median, start by adding an extra column for the **cumulative frequency** if it hasn't already been given. You can do this separately underneath but it makes sense to keep things together and the examiner will be used to seeing this method.

Distance (d miles)	Frequency (f)	CF
$0 < d \leq 1$	12	12
$1 < d \leq 2$	8	20
$2 < d \leq 5$	7	27
$5 < d \leq 10$	5	32

This category goes from 13 to 20 so the 16.5th term will be here.

$\frac{n+1}{2} = \frac{32+1}{2} = 16.5\text{th. term.}$ ✓
The median class is $1 < d \leq 2$ miles. ✓

You find which term will be the median using the formula $\frac{n+1}{2}$. The cumulative frequency column of the table shows the last value in each category and is used to find which category has the median in.

Statistics

The estimated mean distance students live from the school is 2.5 miles. A student was off when Mr Nyembo collected his data. This student lives 5.5 miles away from the school. Anka and Brad work out the new estimated mean.

Anka	Brad			
$\frac{2.5 + 5.5}{2}$	Distance (d miles)	Frequency (f)	Midpoint (x)	fx
	$0 < d \leqslant 1$	12	0.5	$12 \times 0.5 = 6$
$= \frac{8}{2}$	$1 < d \leqslant 2$	8	1.5	$8 \times 1.5 = 12$
	$2 < d \leqslant 5$	7	3.5	$7 \times 3.5 = 24.5$
$= 4$	$5 < d \leqslant 10$	~~5~~6	7.5	$6 \times 7.5 = 45$
	Totals	33		87.5

$$\frac{87.5}{33} = 2.65 \text{ to 2 d.p.}$$

c)   Whose working out is correct? You must explain your answer. *(2 marks)*

Brad is correct because he has put the value into the correct category before working out his estimate of the mean. ✓ ✓

When working out the mean, check that your answer makes sense in the context of the question. Sometimes students divide by the number of categories instead of the total frequencies. That will give a really big answer so you will know you have gone wrong.

8.3 Displaying Data

Stem and Leaf Diagrams

Example 8.3.1

The results of a 500 m race for Year 7 and Year 9 students are to be shown on a back-to-back **stem and leaf diagram**. Complete the diagram using the information below. All times are given in seconds.

Year 7 times:
203, 149, 153, 167, 193, 157, 184, 166, 186, 184, 169, 170, 183, 166, 196, 170, 135, 173, 176, 181, 154, 197, 185, 174, 189, 192, 192, 162, 159, 191

a) Complete the stem and leaf diagram to represent this information. *(3 marks)*

Year 7 times		Year 9 times
	13	9
	14	6 8 9
	15	1 3 4 4 6 7
	16	0 1 2 4 6 8 9 9
	17	3 4 4 7 7
	18	0 1 4 5 6
	19	1 5
	20	2 6

5	13
9	14
9 4 7 3	15
2 6 9 6 7	16
4 6 3 0 0	17
9 5 1 3 4 6 4	18
1 2 2 7 6 3	19
3	20

It is best to put the numbers into the correct line on a copy of the stem and leaf diagram first, and then reorder them on the final diagram.

With a back-to-back stem and leaf diagram, the smallest numbers always go closest to the stem. Don't forget the key, in this case you need a different key for each side.

Year 7 times		Year 9 times
5	13	9
9	14	6 8 9
9 7 4 3	15	1 3 4 4 6 7
9 7 6 6 2	16	0 1 2 4 6 8 9 9
6 4 3 0 0	17	3 4 4 7 7
9 6 5 4 4 3 1	18	0 1 4 5 6
7 6 3 2 2 1	19	1 5
3	20	2 6

Key

5 | 13 represents 135 seconds for the Year 7 times ✓

13 | 9 represents 139 seconds for the Year 9 times

✓ ✓ Fully ordered diagram

b) Zanab says that half of the Year 7 students took over 3 minutes.

Is Zanab correct? *(2 marks)*

3 *minutes is* 3 × 60 = 180 *seconds* 14 *students took over* 180 *seconds.* ✓ *Zanab is wrong because there were* 30 *students, so half would be* 15 *students.* ✓	The question is asked in minutes but the times are given in seconds, so these need to be converted first. Make what you are doing clear and give a conclusion.

Bar Charts

Bar charts are used to show discrete data. One axis will have the categories and the other will show the number of items. Sometimes there will be two things represented for each category, for example male and female. In this case you will need to make sure to include a key.

Example 8.3.2

Aliah counts the number of different types of trees in two parks. Her data is shown in the table.

	Ash	Birch	Cherry	Elm	Sycamore
Abbey Park	5	6	10	4	3
West Park	3	8	7	2	2

a) Draw a suitable diagram or chart for this information that will allow comparison of the two parks. *(4 marks)*

Before drawing in the axes, count the squares of the graph paper and think about the scale you are going to use. Here it makes sense to go up in twos on the y-axis as that makes good use of the space given. On the x-axis there should be a space between each pair of bars.

The two parks can be represented on the graph by colouring in one bar and leaving the other blank. The papers are scanned in for examiners, so do everything in pencil as colours won't be seen.

Include a title, a key and labels on both axes.

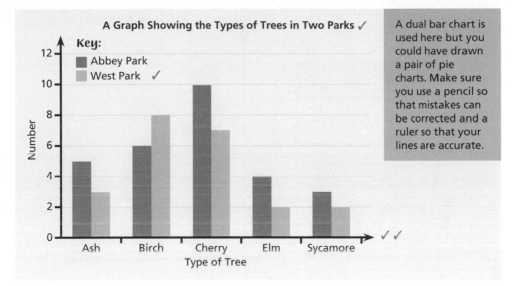

A Graph Showing the Types of Trees in Two Parks ✓

A dual bar chart is used here but you could have drawn a pair of pie charts. Make sure you use a pencil so that mistakes can be corrected and a ruler so that your lines are accurate.

b) Explain how your diagram can be used to compare the number of trees in each park. *(1 mark)*

A comparative bar chart shows the number of each type of tree in the two parks next to each other. ✓

Read the question carefully. You are not being asked to compare the number of trees. You need to explain why your diagram is useful.

Scatter Graphs

Scatter graphs are used to look for a relationship between two sets of data. The data will be in pairs and can be plotted like coordinates. You can also use the graph to state the **correlation** between the two sets of data.

Example 8.3.3

Anna keeps chickens and records how old each chicken is and how many eggs they each lay in a week. The information has been recorded in a table and is shown on the scatter graph.

Statistics

Number of Eggs Laid by Chickens

Age of Chicken (Months)	Number of Eggs per Week
7	6
18	5
20	4
35	2
9	6
11	5
17	4
14	6
28	3

a) Anna made a mistake when plotting one of the points. Correct this mistake. *(1 mark)*

Shown on the diagram (in blue). ✓

b) Describe the relationship between the age of chickens and the number of eggs per week. *(1 mark)*

As the age of the chicken increases, the number of eggs laid per week decreases. ✓

It is important to read the question carefully here as you are being asked for the relationship, not the correlation. When describing relationships you need to use the context in your description. It is fine to also say that it is a negative correlation, but it is the context that will get you the marks.

c) Estimate the number of eggs that would be laid by a chicken that is 38 months old and comment on the reliability of your prediction. *(2 marks)*

From the graph it would be estimated that 1 egg would be laid by a 38 month old chicken. This prediction is extrapolated beyond the range of given values and so may not be very reliable.
✓ Method
✓ Comment

When making predictions, it is a good idea to use a line of best fit. Use your pencil and ruler to draw the line of best fit, then go up to the line from the value you are given and across to find the prediction. Strong students will write a full explanation using the correct terminology.

Pie Charts

Each section of a pie chart represents the proportion of the whole. You will need your protractor for pie chart questions to ensure the angles are measured correctly.

Example 8.3.4

Harrison collected data about the types of fruit students chose at a revision day. He has started to put together a table and a pie chart.
Complete the table and the pie chart to show all of the information. *(5 marks)*

Type of Fruit	Number of Students
Apple	30
Banana	
Grapes	25
Orange	15

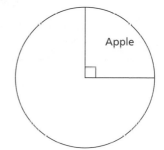

Initially it looks like there isn't enough information but, if you start off as you would for a normal pie chart question and fill in everything you know, you can work out the rest.

$\frac{1}{4}$ of the students chose an apple.

$30 \times 4 = 120$ students in total ✓

$30 + 25 + 15 = 70$

$120 - 70 = 50$ chose a banana ✓

Type of Fruit	Number of Students	Angle
Apple	30	$90°$
Banana	50	$\frac{50}{120} \times 360 = 150°$
Grapes	25	$\frac{25}{120} \times 360 = 75°$
Orange	15	$\frac{15}{120} \times 360 = 45°$
Total	120	$360°$

It is helpful to add an extra column to the table given to put in the angles and to add a row at the bottom for the totals. From the apple section in the pie chart, you can see that 90° represents 30 students. As 90° is a quarter of 360°, you can work out the total number of students and find how many chose a banana. When you have worked out the angles, do a quick check that they add up to 360°.

✓ Method shown

Statistics

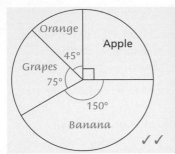

Complete the pie chart using a pencil, ruler and protractor. Don't assume that your last section is correct; measure it to check so that you can detect any earlier mistakes.

Your answers will be scanned in so do not use colours as the examiner will not see them and it can make things difficult to read. Instead, label or use simple patterns to identify each section and show this on a key.

Frequency Polygons

Frequency polygons are used to show the shape of grouped data. Points are plotted at the **midpoint** of the category and joined by straight lines. They do not touch the axes.

Example 8.3.5

Tilda has drawn a frequency polygon showing the lengths of films in a series. She says that half of the films are longer than two and a half hours.

Is Tilda correct? You must explain your answer. *(3 marks)*

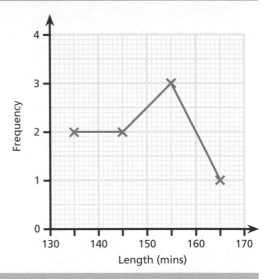

To answer this question, you will need to know how many films there are altogether and how many are longer than two and a half hours.

$2 + 2 + 3 + 1 = 8$ *films altogether* ✓
2 *hours* $= 2 \times 60 = 120$ *minutes*
$120 + 30 = 150$ *minutes* ✓
$3 + 1 = 4$ *that are longer*
$\frac{4}{8} = \frac{1}{2}$
Tilda is correct that half of the films are over two and a half hours long. ✓

The length of films given on the frequency polygon is in minutes, so first you should convert two and a half hours to minutes.

Make sure you have answered the question. Strong students will write this as a full sentence in the context of the question.

Time Series Graphs

A time series graph looks at patterns over time and is particularly useful for data that might be seasonal, where you are looking for trends. For example, ice-cream sales are likely to be much higher in summer months so comparing sales in December to those in June wouldn't be very helpful, but looking at sales for three years split up by season could help to identify trends.

Example 8.3.6

Emma works in an office and wants to find out about how many people walk or cycle to work. She has collected information over two years and wants to present it as a time series graph.

	Walk
Spring (2015)	40
Summer (2015)	41
Autumn (2015)	39
Winter (2015)	33
Spring (2016)	39
Summer (2016)	44
Autumn (2016)	41
Winter (2016)	36

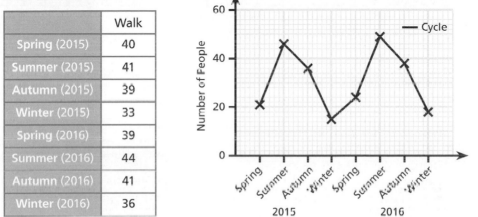

a) Draw on the information for people who walk to work. *(3 marks)*

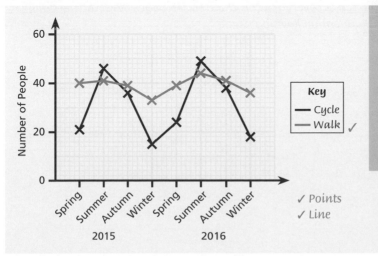

Plot the points in line with the labels for the seasons. Use a pencil and have a rubber ready in case you go wrong. The points should then be joined with straight lines using a ruler. Don't forget to include a key.

✓ Points
✓ Line

b) At which point is the difference between the number of cyclists and the number of people walking the highest? *(2 marks)*

Spring 2015: $40 - 21 = 19$

Winter 2015: $33 - 15 = 18$

Spring 2016: $39 - 24 = 15$

Winter 2016: $36 - 18 = 18$

The biggest difference is in spring 2015 when there were 19 more people walking than cycling. ✓ ✓

From the graph you can see that the biggest differences are in spring and winter so these are the differences to check. You might not need to write out each of the calculations if it is clear on the graph, but it is often helpful and makes sure your working out is clear.

c) Describe the trends in the number of people cycling and walking to work. *(2 marks)*

The number of people walking to work remains similar over the year with a small drop in the winter. ✓

The number of people cycling in 2016 is slightly higher for each season than in 2015. The number of people cycling to work is much lower in the winter than in the summer. ✓

There are two marks for this question, so you should be making at least two comparisons. It is a good idea to make a comparison for each data set if two data sets are given, so here there would be one mark for writing about the number of people who walk and another for those who cycle.

For more on the topics covered in this chapter, see pages 88–91 of the Collins Edexcel Maths Foundation Revision Guide.

Statistics: Key Notes

- If asked about a sampling technique, you are looking for any sources of bias. Try to think about parts of the population that may be missed out or over-represented.
- Data can be discrete (meaning that it takes distinct values which could be numbers or categorical, e.g. red, blue, orange, etc.) or continuous (meaning that it can take any value over a continuous range).
- The range measures how spread out data is and is found by subtracting the smallest value from the largest.
- The median is found by putting all values in order and finding the middle ($\frac{n+1}{2}$th) term. If there are two middle terms, then they are added together and halved.
  - To find the median from a table, add a cumulative frequency column to help find the middle term.
- The mode is the value that occurs the most often. A data set can have more than one mode or no mode.
- The mean is the total of all values divided by the number of values.
  - To find the mean from a table, multiply each value in the first column by its frequency. Then find the sum of these products and divide by the sum of the frequencies. This can be written as mean $= \frac{\Sigma fx}{\Sigma f}$
  - If the data is grouped, the mean will be an estimate and midpoints should be used for the x value.
- There are a number of ways data can be displayed. Use a pencil and ruler to draw graphs and make sure you have labels on the axes with a key if necessary.
- Bar charts are used for discrete data. The height of the bars shows the frequency and the bars do not touch.
- Scatter graphs show the relationship between two variables.
  - If you are asked to describe the relationship between two variables, your answer should be in the context of the question. For example, as the temperature increases, so do ice-cream sales.
  - If the question asks for the type of correlation, you should say whether it is positive (both variables are increasing), negative (as one increases, the other decreases) or if there is no correlation.
  - When using a scatter graph for estimations, **interpolation** is within the range of given values so is likely to be reliable. **Extrapolation** is estimating outside the range of values and therefore may be unreliable.
- Pie charts show the proportion of each category at a glance. Each section is a proportion of 360°.
- For frequency polygons, the frequency for each group is plotted at the midpoint of the group.
- Time series graphs show trends over time. The points are plotted in line with the label and joined with straight lines.

9   Transferable Skills

Mathematics is valued not just for the techniques and procedures learned but also for the transferable skills that are developed. This section looks at some general exam hints and tips, as well as the types of questions in which you will need to use the mathematics you have learned in different contexts. These are the AO2 and AO3 questions that will require you to use skills from different areas of mathematics. Most importantly, you will need strong reasoning skills and will need to give clear explanations.

9.1 Exam Hints and Tips

- Read the question before, during and after answering.
- Stay calm. You won't be asked to do things that are impossible (though hype on social media may lead you to question this!). Remember, there are a lot of marks on every question for method and intermediate answers, so do what you can, even if you don't know how it might help you reach the final answer.
- Always consider earlier parts to questions and whether they make later parts simpler.
- If the question needs multiple steps to solve it, write a brief plan of what you intend to do. This can help keep you on track or think about what you are trying to achieve in smaller steps, rather than considering the entire thing in one go.
- If the question has a diagram, add all the information to it as you go along. Redraw diagrams if they are getting over-complicated to show the part you need to focus on.
- Mark your answer in some way (such as a pencilled star on the page) if you feel it is worth coming back to and if there is time. Fight the urge to cross something out if you think you have made a mistake.
- You should be spending roughly one minute per mark; some will take less time and some more. Don't spend too long trying to get one or two early marks and then run out of time for big questions later on!
- When you think you have finished the question, do a final check:
  - Make sure you have answered the question. It is easy to find x, write it on the dotted line and move on, but were you asked to find x or was that an intermediate step?
  - Does the question ask you to round to a specific number of decimal places or significant figures?
  - Is your answer in the correct form? Have you used the correct units?
  - If the question says to give your answer in its simplest form, there will be an easy mark for this so make sure you have simplified fully. This is especially important for fractions, algebra and surds.
  - Check the context of the question to see if your answer makes sense. If it doesn't, you probably need to check your working out.

9.2 Answering AO2 Questions

Edexcel describes AO2 (Assessment Objective 2) as 'about reasoning, interpreting and communicating mathematically'. This assessment objective will be worth 25% at foundation tier and is likely to test mathematical skills from across the syllabus, sometimes with more than one topic in a question.

AO2 can be tested in different ways and an example question is given for each, though the boundaries are quite blurred and questions may draw on a number of the skills described in the assessment objective.

Making Deductions, Inferences and Drawing Conclusions from Mathematical Information

You could be given mathematical information in a standard context, such as finding an angle from given values, or you may need to use the mathematical information to solve a problem in context as shown below.

Example 9.2.1

Monika makes handmade bead bracelets. She uses the formula Price $- 3.12 + 0.8b$ to work out the cost of bracelets in pounds, where b is the number of beads used. A customer from Italy ordered a bracelet and paid €11.20. The exchange rate was €1 = £0.85

How many beads did the bracelet have? (3 marks)

Working	Explanation
$\begin{array}{cc} € & £ \\ 1 & 0.85 \end{array}$	The formula is for the price in pounds and the amount paid is in euros, so first convert to pounds.
$11.20 \times 0.85 = 9.52 \checkmark$	Using the formula given, you can set up an equation to solve.
$3.12 + 0.8b = 9.52$ $-3.12 \qquad -3.12$ $\dfrac{0.8b}{0.8} = \dfrac{6.40}{0.8}$ $b = 8 \checkmark$	There are decimals which makes it look more complicated, but you follow exactly the same rules as normal.
The bracelet had 8 beads. $\checkmark$	Write your answer clearly at the end to make the examiner's life easier.

Constructing Chains of Reasoning to Achieve a Given Result

Chains of reasoning is basically talking about having clear working out that can be easily followed. You are showing your reasoning at each stage so that someone else would be able to understand why you have done calculations or decided things.

Example 9.2.2

Corinne and Rene are making badges to sell at their school fair. There are three different badges and they think some will be more popular than others, so they decide on the following rules:

- There should be twice as many of badge 2 as badge 1.
- There should be 20 more of badge 3 than badge 1.

They buy a pack of 100 badges for £8.20 plus VAT at 20% and sell the badges for 25p each. All of the type 3 badges are sold and $\frac{3}{4}$ of types 1 and 2 are sold.

How much profit do Corinne and Rene make? *(5 marks)*

Cost of badges:

$8.20 \times 1.2 = £9.84$ ✓

> To find the price with the additional 20% for VAT, the multiplier 1.2 is used as it is 120%. You could also find 20% using a different method and add it on.

Number of badges:

Type 1: b

Type 2: $2b$

> Label what you are doing at each stage to keep things organised.

Type 3: $b + 20$

$b + 2b + b + 20 = 100$

$\qquad 4b + 20 = 100$

$\qquad\quad -20 \quad -20$

$\qquad\quad \dfrac{4b}{4} = \dfrac{80}{4}$

$\qquad\qquad b = 20$ ✓

> An equation can be formed from the information given to find the number of each type of badges.

Type 1: 20

Type 2: $2 \times 20 = 40$

Type 3: $20 + 20 = 40$

Number sold:

$\frac{3}{4} \times (20 + 40) = \frac{3}{4} \times 60 = 45$

$45 + 40 = 85$ in total ✓

Money taken:

$85 \times 0.25 = £21.25$ ✓

Profit:

$21.25 - 9.84 = £11.41$ ✓

Interpreting and Communicating Information Accurately

Similarly to the previous concept, it is important that your work can be easily understood but here it is more likely that you will be given information in a way that requires you to do a bit more thinking.

Example 9.2.3

Andrea is a personal trainer. She offers discounts on sessions with more than one person as shown opposite.

Three friends have enquired about the cost of a session: Emily says that she would like to train every two days, Ines would like to train every three days and Taiwo wants to train every five days.

Personal Training
£18 per session

$\frac{1}{6}$ off for 2 people training together

$\frac{1}{3}$ off for groups of 3 or more

Andrea is looking for a way to show the cost of their sessions for the first 30 days. Work out this cost, making all calculations clear. *(5 marks)*

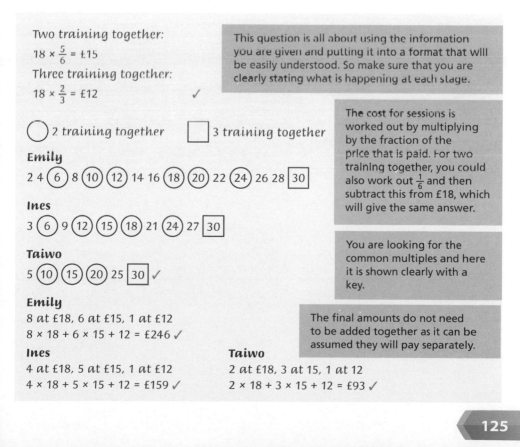

Two training together:

$18 \times \frac{5}{6} = £15$

Three training together:

$18 \times \frac{2}{3} = £12$ ✓

This question is all about using the information you are given and putting it into a format that will be easily understood. So make sure that you are clearly stating what is happening at each stage.

◯ 2 training together   ▢ 3 training together

Emily

2 4 ⑥ 8 ⑩ ⑫ 14 16 ⑱ ⑳ 22 ㉔ 26 28 [30]

Ines

3 ⑥ 9 ⑫ ⑮ ⑱ 21 ㉔ 27 [30]

Taiwo

5 ⑩ ⑮ ⑳ 25 [30] ✓

The cost for sessions is worked out by multiplying by the fraction of the price that is paid. For two training together, you could also work out $\frac{1}{6}$ and then subtract this from £18, which will give the same answer.

You are looking for the common multiples and here it is shown clearly with a key.

Emily

8 at £18, 6 at £15, 1 at £12

$8 \times 18 + 6 \times 15 + 12 = £246$ ✓

The final amounts do not need to be added together as it can be assumed they will pay separately.

Ines

4 at £18, 5 at £15, 1 at £12

$4 \times 18 + 5 \times 15 + 12 = £159$ ✓

Taiwo

2 at £18, 3 at 15, 1 at 12

$2 \times 18 + 3 \times 15 + 12 = £93$ ✓

Presenting Arguments and Proofs

A proof is a mathematical argument whereby you set out steps that can be followed to go from the information given to a conclusion. Sometimes this conclusion will already be given and you are asked to show that it is true.

Diagram not drawn to scale

Example 9.2.4

The circle shown has its centre at point C. In degrees, angle ABC is $3a$ and angle ACB is $8a + 40$.

Show that triangle ACD is equilateral. *(5 marks)*

Angle BAC is the same as angle ABC because the triangle is isosceles.

$3a + 3a + 8a + 40 = 180$

$14a + 40 = 180$

$-40 \quad -40$

$\frac{14a}{14} = \frac{140}{14}$

$a = 10$ ✓

$3 \times 10 = 30°$ $8 \times 10 + 40 = 120°$ ✓

Angle ACD $180 - 120 = 60°$

Angles on a straight line = 180°

Angle CAD $90 - 30 = 60°$

The angle in a semicircle is a right angle. ✓

Angle ADC $180 - 2 \times 60 = 60°$

Angles in a triangle = 180° ✓

All three angles are 60°, therefore it is an equilateral triangle. ✓

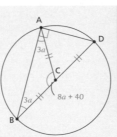

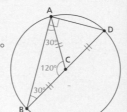

A question asking you to 'prove' or 'show' means you need to work from the information given towards the thing you are trying to prove. In other words, you cannot use the fact that the triangle is equilateral – you have to work towards showing that.

The diagram doesn't have much information so start by adding everything you know. You might not need it yet (or even at all) but it is good to have as much detail as you can on there.

When describing angles, you follow the path given and it is the angle in the middle that is being referred to.

Now that you know the angles in degrees, they can be added on as well. If your original diagram becomes too cluttered, you can always redraw the diagram. It doesn't need to be a beautiful drawing, so long as it is useful.

Give a reason for everything you do.

Assessing the Validity of an Argument and Critically Evaluating a Given Way of Presenting Information

With these kinds of questions you are looking for mistakes or wrong information. Statistics is a common context. You will need to identify and explain the problems convincingly, not just say that they are wrong.

Example 9.2.5

Lois has used the graph below to write an article about the recent election. Her headline is shown below the graph. As the editor, you need to check each journalist's work and provide feedback. Write down two things that are wrong with the information. *(2 marks)*

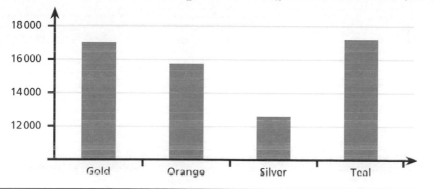

> **Victory for the new Teal Party, which got more than double the number of votes as the previous winners, the Silver Party**

The headline is misleading. Although it looks like the Teal Party did much better than the Silver Party, the graph does not start at 0 so the difference is actually much smaller. The graph needs to make it clear that the scale does not start at 0. The axes should also have labels on to show what is being represented. ✓ ✓

9.3 Answering AO3 Questions

Edexcel describes AO3 as 'about solving problems with a much greater focus on solving non-routine problems in mathematical and non-mathematical contexts'. These questions can be tricky to answer, often because they are asking you to use more than one area of mathematics. They also require you to apply a great deal of common sense as the questions will generally be set in a context. There will usually be more than one way to answer the question but in all cases having clear, easy-to-follow methods will be very important.

Translating Problems in Mathematical or Non-mathematical Contexts into a Process or a Series of Mathematical Processes

With these questions you will be given a situation from which you need to draw out the mathematics. You may be given more information than you need and have to work out the important parts.

Example 9.3.1

Callum has an appointment at Binary Road, which is 8 miles from his house. His appointment is at 11am. He takes 10 minutes to walk to the Latitude Lane bus stop, which is half a mile from his house. When he gets there at 10:10, he sees the sign below.

Broad Street	09:14	09:36	09:58	10:19
Latitude Lane	09:29	09:51	10:13	10:34
Chapel Street	09:37	09:59	10:21	10:42
White Road	09:50	10:12	10:34	10:55
Binary Road	10:04	10:26	10:48	11:09
Garden Row	10:12	10:34	10:56	11:17
South Crescent	10:28	10:50	11:12	11:33

Buses are diverted via Division Street so will take up to an extra 15 minutes.

Apologies for the delay.

Callum goes home to get his bike so that he can cycle to Binary Road at 12 mph. Should he do this instead? *(2 marks)*

Bus: 10:48 + 15 minutes = 11:03

Walking home: 10 minutes

Cycling:
$T = \frac{D}{S} = \frac{8}{12} = \frac{2}{3}$ hours

$\frac{2}{3} \times 60 = 40$ minutes ✓

Total 50 minutes so he would arrive at 11am if he cycled.

He should cycle because then he will get there at 11 am, just in time for his appointment. ✓

Each section of the journey is labelled clearly to avoid any confusion.

The information about the bus can be read from the table. Use your ruler to help read from the table if it helps.

Don't forget to include the time taken for him to walk back home to get his bike.

Your final line should answer the question given, with reference to the calculations you have done.

Making and Using Connections Between Different Parts of Mathematics

Questions can make links between different areas of mathematics to make you think about things in a different context. Algebra comes into almost all areas of mathematics and Chapter 4 contains many more examples of connections. Usually the individual steps will be fairly straightforward but knowing where to start can be difficult. A good idea is to look at everything you know about the situation and make a start on your answer, but be ready to try a different tactic if your first doesn't work.

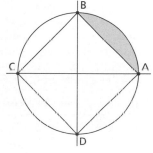

Example 9.3.2

The circle shown opposite has its centre at the origin. The points A, B, C and D represent the intersections of the circle with the coordinate axes. Point A is (4, 0).

Find the shaded area, giving your answer in the form $a(\pi - b)$. *(4 marks)*

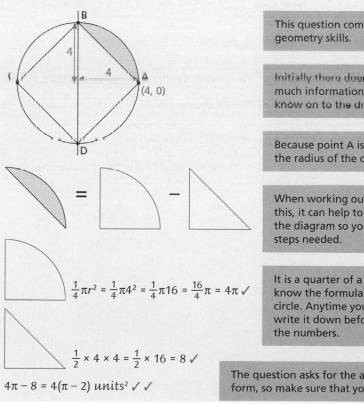

This question combines algebra and geometry skills.

Initially there doesn't seem to be very much information but draw what you know on to the diagram.

Because point A is given, you can find the radius of the circle.

When working out area questions like this, it can help to redraw sections of the diagram so you can see clearly the steps needed.

$$\frac{1}{4}\pi r^2 = \frac{1}{4}\pi 4^2 = \frac{1}{4}\pi 16 = \frac{16}{4}\pi = 4\pi \checkmark$$

It is a quarter of a circle; you should know the formula for the area of a circle. Anytime you use a formula, write it down before substituting in the numbers.

$$\frac{1}{2} \times 4 \times 4 = \frac{1}{2} \times 16 = 8 \checkmark$$

$$4\pi - 8 = 4(\pi - 2) \ units^2 \checkmark\checkmark$$

The question asks for the answer in a particular form, so make sure that you have done this.

Evaluating Methods Used and Results Obtained

When you are evaluating, you are considering the good and bad points of the methods and results.

Example 9.3.3

Alena is saving money. Alena decided that each week she will check the serial number of the first £5 note she gets and if it ends with a prime number she will spend it. Otherwise she will put the £5 note into her savings jar. She says that by the end of week 50, she will have saved £150. Her calculations are shown.

$$0\ 1\ 2\ 3\ 4\ 5\ 6\ 7\ 8\ 9$$
$$P(\text{not prime}) = \frac{6}{10} = \frac{3}{5}$$
$$\frac{3}{5} \times 50 = 30$$
$$30 \times £5 = £150$$

Explain whether she is correct. *(2 marks)*

Alena's calculations are correct. However, this is an estimated value. She is unlikely to get exactly 30 notes with a non-prime final digit, so she will probably have more or less than £150. ✓ ✓

A good answer will be written in full, coherent sentences to get your point across well.

Interpreting Results in the Context of the Given Problem

Context is important in a lot of questions because you should ensure that the answer makes sense for the given situation. For these types of question, you will need to use your results to solve a problem or answer a question.

Example 9.3.4

Paul is making cheese and onion pasties. The pasties will be triangles made by folding 20 cm squares in half diagonally. Each pasty will have 150 g of filling containing cheese, onion and potato in the ratio 3 : 3 : 4. The pastry should be rolled to a thickness of 3 mm. The ingredients he has bought are shown below.

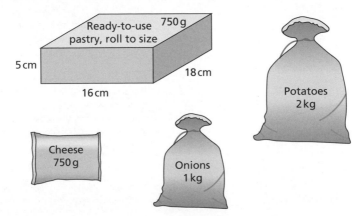

What is the maximum number of pasties Paul can make? *(6 marks)*

There is an awful lot of information in this question but it can be broken down into small steps. Make it clear which part of the question you are working on so that you can check your working out quickly and bring all the information together at the end.

Pastry:

$5 × 16 × 18 = 1440\,cm^3$ in the block

$0.3 × 20 × 20 = 120\,cm^3$ needed for each pasty ✓

$1440 ÷ 120 = 12$ pasties ✓

It doesn't matter in which order you tackle this question. Here the pastry is dealt with first but you could have done the filling first. Check the units as the thickness of the pastry when re-rolled is given in millimetres and everything else is in centimetres. Convert everything to either millimetres or centimetres.

Filling: amounts needed per pasty

	Cheese	Onion	Potato	Total
×15	3	3	4	10
	45g	45g	60g	150g

Set up your ratios clearly and double-check that, when you have found the amounts for each of the ingredients, they add up to 150g.

Cheese:

$750 ÷ 45 = 16.\dot{6}$ so 16 maximum

Although $16.\dot{6}$ would normally round up to 17, in this case it rounds down as you cannot have $0.\dot{6}$ of a pasty!

Onion:

$1000 ÷ 45 = 22.\dot{2}$ so 22 maximum ✓

Polato:

$2000 ÷ 60 = 33.\dot{3}$ so 33 maximum ✓

Again the units are important as the amount of potato and onions is given in kilograms and needs to be converted to grams.

The maximum number of pasties Paul can make is 12. ✓

Write the answer clearly in the context of the question.

All the calculations are done but you haven't finished yet as you need to make sure you have answered the question. Looking at all of the amounts, you need to choose the smallest.

Evaluating Solutions to Identify How They May Have Been Affected by Assumptions Made

Assumptions are things that have been taken to be true which may not necessarily be true or could have been interpreted differently. You are trying to find and explain any potential problems.

Example 9.3.5

Ala lives in a shared house with three other people and he is in charge of the gas bill. They share the cost of the gas equally. There are two tariff options available shown below. He has the meter readings from the last day of each month in the previous year.

They use more gas in the winter than in the summer but they choose to pay a fixed amount per month and this is based on the average amount of fuel used per month so that the extra cost in the winter is spread over the whole year. VAT of 5% is charged on all energy bills.

Initial Reading	1781		
January	2591	July	5453
February	3257	August	5741
March	3815	September	6083
April	4283	October	6515
May	4769	November	7019
June	5147	December	7595

Deal 1
11.55p standing charge per day
9.55p per unit used

Deal 2
12.15p standing charge per day
8.75p per unit used

How much would each person save per month by being on the cheaper deal? State any assumptions you have made. *(5 marks)*

Amount used over the year
7595 − 1781 = 5814

If there are two or more things to compare, it can help to split the page so that calculations are clearly separated.

Deal 1	**Deal 2**
Cost for units used:	
5814 × 9.55 = 55 523.7	5814 × 8.75 = 50 872.5
Standing charge:	
365 × 11.55 = 4215.75	365 × 12.15 = 4434.75
Total:	
55 523.7 + 4215.75 = 59 739.45	50 872.5 + 4434.75 = 55 307.25 ✓
VAT:	
59 739.45 × 1.05 = 62 726.4225p	55 307.25 × 1.05 = 58 072.6125p
= £627.26 *(per year)*	= £580.73
627.26 ÷ 12 = £52.27 *(per month)*	580.73 ÷ 12 = £48.39 ✓
52.27 ÷ 4 = £13.07 *(per person)*	48.39 ÷ 4 = £12.10 ✓

Check the units. In this case, it has been in pence so far but now it makes sense to change to using pounds.

Difference 13.07 − 12.10 = 97p
They can save 97p a month each on deal 2. ✓
It is assumed that they will use the same amount of gas next year.
It is assumed that prices remain fixed for the year.
It is assumed that there are 365 days, so it is not a leap year. ✓

Your two answers should be similar. It would be unusual to get two very different answers so, if you do, check your working out carefully.

You may have worked this out differently, in which case you would have different assumptions.

Revision Sheet and Formulae to Learn

A formulae page will not be given at the front of the exam paper, so if you are given a formula it will be as part of the question. The notes below highlight some of the things to look out for to help you avoid some of the common pitfalls.

Formulae You Will Be Given

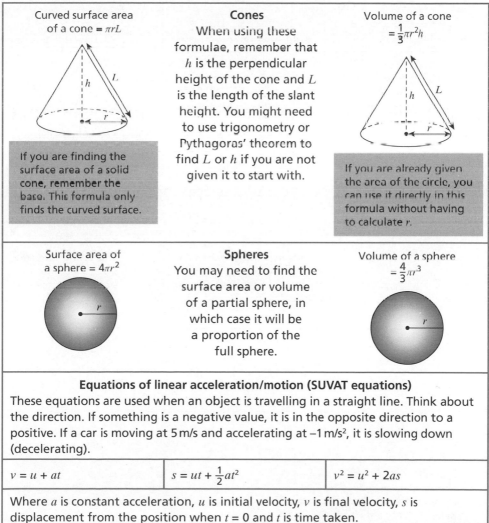

Curved surface area of a cone = $\pi r L$

Cones

When using these formulae, remember that h is the perpendicular height of the cone and L is the length of the slant height. You might need to use trigonometry or Pythagoras' theorem to find L or h if you are not given it to start with.

Volume of a cone $= \frac{1}{3}\pi r^2 h$

If you are finding the surface area of a solid cone, remember the base. This formula only finds the curved surface.

If you are already given the area of the circle, you can use it directly in this formula without having to calculate r.

Surface area of a sphere = $4\pi r^2$

Spheres

You may need to find the surface area or volume of a partial sphere, in which case it will be a proportion of the full sphere.

Volume of a sphere $= \frac{4}{3}\pi r^3$

Equations of linear acceleration/motion (SUVAT equations)

These equations are used when an object is travelling in a straight line. Think about the direction. If something is a negative value, it is in the opposite direction to a positive. If a car is moving at 5 m/s and accelerating at −1 m/s², it is slowing down (decelerating).

$v = u + at$	$s = ut + \frac{1}{2}at^2$	$v^2 = u^2 + 2as$

Where a is constant acceleration, u is initial velocity, v is final velocity, s is displacement from the position when $t = 0$ and t is time taken.

Formulae You Need to Know

These are some of the key formulae that you need to know. There are some useful suggestions for remembering formulae in Chapter 2 but plenty of practice is needed.

Area and Volume

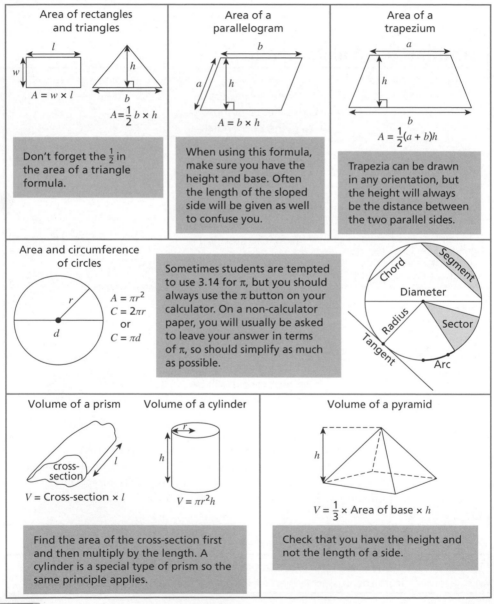

Area of rectangles and triangles

$A = w \times l$

$A = \frac{1}{2} b \times h$

Don't forget the $\frac{1}{2}$ in the area of a triangle formula.

Area of a parallelogram

$A = b \times h$

When using this formula, make sure you have the height and base. Often the length of the sloped side will be given as well to confuse you.

Area of a trapezium

$A = \frac{1}{2}(a + b)h$

Trapezia can be drawn in any orientation, but the height will always be the distance between the two parallel sides.

Area and circumference of circles

$A = \pi r^2$
$C = 2\pi r$
or
$C = \pi d$

Sometimes students are tempted to use 3.14 for π, but you should always use the π button on your calculator. On a non-calculator paper, you will usually be asked to leave your answer in terms of π, so should simplify as much as possible.

Chord   Segment   Diameter   Radius   Sector   Tangent   Arc

Volume of a prism

cross-section

$V = \text{Cross-section} \times l$

Volume of a cylinder

$V = \pi r^2 h$

Find the area of the cross-section first and then multiply by the length. A cylinder is a special type of prism so the same principle applies.

Volume of a pyramid

$V = \frac{1}{3} \times \text{Area of base} \times h$

Check that you have the height and not the length of a side.

Trigonometry

For all trigonometry questions, you should check that your calculator is in the correct mode. It is good practice to reset your calculator at the start of the exam and you should know how to do this without instructions in case you accidentally put it into a different mode in the exam.

Any time you put in a trigonometric function of an angle (sine, cosine or tangent), many calculators will automatically insert a bracket. Remember to close this bracket once you have keyed in the angle. If you get an error, it is usually because you are trying to do sine⁻¹ or cosine⁻¹ of a number greater than 1. Go back and check your working out.

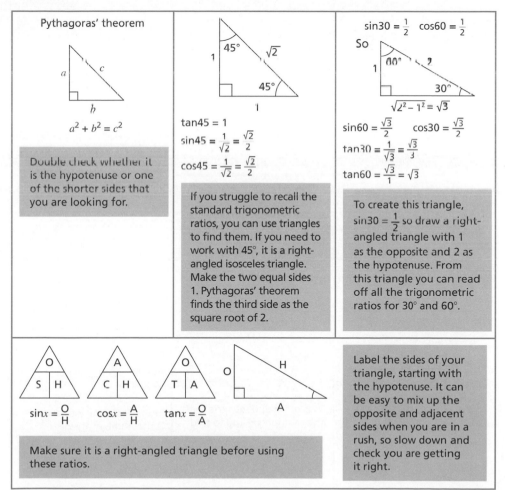

Pythagoras' theorem

$$a^2 + b^2 = c^2$$

Double check whether it is the hypotenuse or one of the shorter sides that you are looking for.

$$\tan45 = 1$$
$$\sin45 = \frac{1}{\sqrt{2}} = \frac{\sqrt{2}}{2}$$
$$\cos45 = \frac{1}{\sqrt{2}} = \frac{\sqrt{2}}{2}$$

If you struggle to recall the standard trigonometric ratios, you can use triangles to find them. If you need to work with 45°, it is a right-angled isosceles triangle. Make the two equal sides 1. Pythagoras' theorem finds the third side as the square root of 2.

$$\sin30 = \frac{1}{2} \quad \cos60 = \frac{1}{2}$$

So

$$\sqrt{2^2 - 1^2} = \sqrt{3}$$

$$\sin60 = \frac{\sqrt{3}}{2} \quad \cos30 = \frac{\sqrt{3}}{2}$$
$$\tan30 = \frac{1}{\sqrt{3}} = \frac{\sqrt{3}}{3}$$
$$\tan60 = \frac{\sqrt{3}}{1} = \sqrt{3}$$

To create this triangle, $\sin30 = \frac{1}{2}$ so draw a right-angled triangle with 1 as the opposite and 2 as the hypotenuse. From this triangle you can read off all the trigonometric ratios for 30° and 60°.

$$\sin x = \frac{O}{H} \quad \cos x = \frac{A}{H} \quad \tan x = \frac{O}{A}$$

Make sure it is a right-angled triangle before using these ratios.

Label the sides of your triangle, starting with the hypotenuse. It can be easy to mix up the opposite and adjacent sides when you are in a rush, so slow down and check you are getting it right.

Angle Reasoning (and Parallel Lines)

You need to be able to recognise the following rules and be able to explain what you have done and why. Using the correct vocabulary is important.

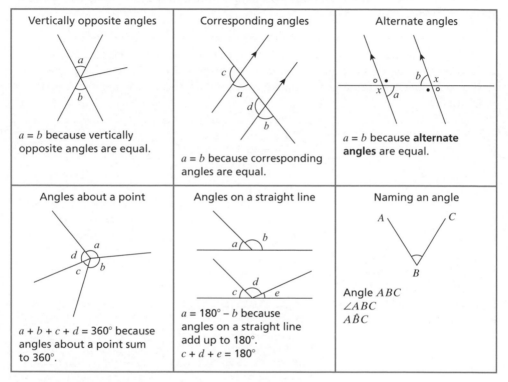

Vertically opposite angles	Corresponding angles	Alternate angles
$a = b$ because vertically opposite angles are equal.	$a = b$ because corresponding angles are equal.	$a = b$ because **alternate angles** are equal.
Angles about a point	Angles on a straight line	Naming an angle
$a + b + c + d = 360°$ because angles about a point sum to 360°.	$a = 180° - b$ because angles on a straight line add up to 180°. $c + d + e = 180°$	Angle ABC $\angle ABC$ $A\hat{B}C$

Angles in Regular Polygons

There are three different ways to work out angles in an n-sided regular polygon.

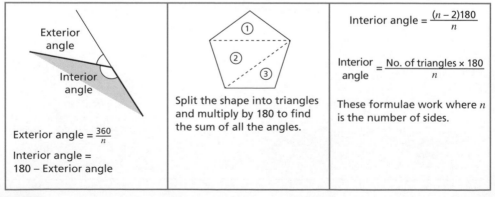

Exterior angle

Interior angle

Exterior angle $= \frac{360}{n}$

Interior angle = 180 – Exterior angle

Split the shape into triangles and multiply by 180 to find the sum of all the angles.

Interior angle $= \frac{(n-2)180}{n}$

$\dfrac{\text{Interior}}{\text{angle}} = \dfrac{\text{No. of triangles} \times 180}{n}$

These formulae work where n is the number of sides.

Measure Conversions

If you are asked to convert between metric and imperial measures, these will be given as part of the question. You will need to know conversions between common metric units.

Length	Weight	Capacity
10 mm = 1 cm	1000 g = 1 kg	1000 ml = 1 l
100 cm = 1 m		
1000 m = 1 km		

Compound Measures

$Speed = \dfrac{Distance}{Time}$ $Density = \dfrac{Mass}{Volume}$ $Pressure = \dfrac{Force}{Area}$

When dealing with different measures, check the units carefully and convert if necessary before doing your calculations.

Laws of Indices

$a^n \longleftarrow$ Power

Base

$a^n \times a^m = a^{n+m}$

$a^n \div a^m = a^{n-m}$

$(a^n)^m = a^{n \times m}$

$\dfrac{1}{a^n} = a^{-n}$

$a^0 = 1$

Anything to the power of 0 is 1.

Make sure that the bases are the same before you apply these laws.

If the powers are numbers and you aren't sure, try writing it out.

Algebraic Graphs

There are four types of graphs that you should be able to recognise. They are shown below along with the general form of their equations.

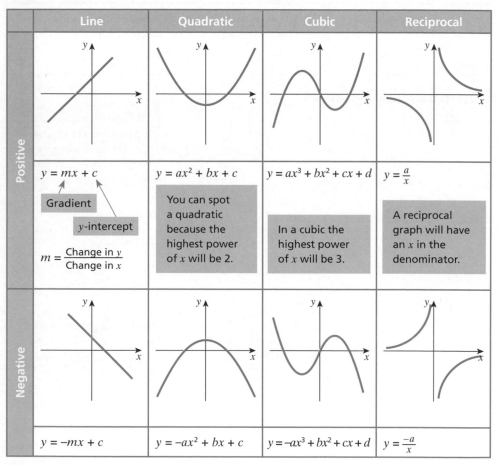

	Line	Quadratic	Cubic	Reciprocal
Positive	$y = mx + c$ Gradient y-intercept $m = \dfrac{\text{Change in } y}{\text{Change in } x}$	$y = ax^2 + bx + c$ You can spot a quadratic because the highest power of x will be 2.	$y = ax^3 + bx^2 + cx + d$ In a cubic the highest power of x will be 3.	$y = \dfrac{a}{x}$ A reciprocal graph will have an x in the denominator.
Negative	$y = -mx + c$	$y = -ax^2 + bx + c$	$y = -ax^3 + bx^2 + cx + d$	$y = \dfrac{-a}{x}$

Averages and Range

Mean $= \dfrac{\text{Sum of the values}}{\text{Number of values}}$	Median is the middle number when the values are in order.	Mode occurs the most often.	Range = Largest value – Smallest value

alternate angles a pair of equal angles formed when a pair (or more) of parallel lines are crossed by the same straight line (the transversal); the alternate angles are on opposite sides of the transversal

arc a curve forming part of the circumference of a circle

arithmetic sequence a sequence with a common first difference between consecutive terms

asymptote a line that a curve continually approaches but never touches

BIDMAS an acronym that helps you remember the order of operations. Brackets, Indices and roots, Division and Multiplication, Addition and Subtraction

binomial a polynomial with two parts; the sum or difference between two algebraic terms

centre of enlargement the point from which the enlargement happens

centre of rotation the point around which a shape is rotated

chord a line joining two points on the circumference of a circle

class interval the width of a class or group, e.g. $0\,g <$ mass of spider $\leqslant 10\,g$

coefficient a constant multiplying an algebraic term that can be either a number or a letter (often a, b, c).

compound interest interest that accrues from the initial deposit plus the interest added on at the end of each year

conditional probability the probability that an event will occur given that another event has already occurred

congruent exactly alike in shape and size

constant a number, either known or unknown, within an algebraic expression that doesn't change

constant of proportionality the constant value of the ratio of two proportional quantities x and y; if $y \propto x$, then $y = kx$ (k is the constant of proportionality)

correlation the relationship between the numerical values of two variables, e.g. there is a negative correlation between the age and the value of cars

corresponding angles a pair of equal angles formed when a pair (or more) of parallel lines are crossed by the same straight line (the transversal); the corresponding angles are both on the same side of the transversal

cross-section/cross-sectional a shape/ surface created when a cut is made through a mathematical object parallel to its 'base' / perpendicular to its central axis

cube number the product of three integers that are equal, e.g. $2^3 = 2 \times 2 \times 2 = 8$ so 8 is a cube number

depreciate/depreciation/depreciated a decrease in the value of something; generally expressed as a proportional reduction in value as a percentage

direct proportion two values or measurements may vary in direct proportion, i.e. if one doubles, then so does the other; this can be represented as a linear graph that passes through the origin with equation of the form $y = mx$ (the symbol $\propto$ means proportional)

empty set a set containing no objects (members)

enlargement a transformation of a plane figure or solid object that increases (or decreases) the size of the figure or object by a scale factor but leaves it the same shape; a scale factor of $-1 < f < 1, f \neq 0$ results in the shape getting smaller

equation a number sentence where one side is equal to the other

expression a statement that uses letters as well as numbers

exterior angle an angle outside a polygon, formed when a side is extended

extrapolation estimations that are beyond the range of given values, meaning they may be unreliable

factor a number that can be represented algebraically and can divide the whole to leave either an integer value or an expression without fractions

factorisation finding one or more factors of a given number or algebraic expression

Fibonacci sequence a number sequence found in nature; the sequence is formed by adding the previous two terms;

$u_{n+2} = u_n + u_{n+1}$

finite set a set which has an exact number of members

formula an equation that enables you to convert, or find a value, using other known values, e.g.

Area = Length × Width

frequency tree see **tree diagram**

function a relationship between a set of inputs and a set of outputs

geometric sequence a sequence with a common ratio

gradient the measure of the steepness of a slope: $\frac{\text{Vertical change}}{\text{Horizontal change}}$ or *'how many 'up' for every 1 space to the right'*, bearing in mind that −1 up is the same as 1 down

identity similar to an equation but true for all values of the variable(s); the identity symbol is $\equiv$, e.g. $2(x + 3) \equiv 2x + 6$

independent events two events are independent if the outcome of one event is not affected by the outcome of the other event, e.g. flipping a coin and rolling a dice

index (also known as **power** or **exponent**; plural: **indices**) the small digit to the top right of a number that tells you the number of times a number is multiplied by itself, e.g. 5^4 is $5 \times 5 \times 5 \times 5$; the index is 4

inequality a statement showing two quantities that are not equal

Key symbols:

$x \neq y$	x and y are not equal
$x \leqslant y$	x is less than, or equal to, y
$x \geqslant y$	x is greater than, or equal to, y
$x < y$	x is less than y
$x > y$	x is greater than y

infinite set a set which continues forever, i.e. it has no end number

intercept the point where a line or graph crosses an axis

interest (see also **compound interest**) a percentage increase, generally associated with money invested in an account

interior angle an angle between the sides inside a polygon

interpolation an estimation of values between known discrete data points; as the estimation is within given values, it is likely to be reliable

intersection the point at which two or more lines cross

inverse (indirect) proportion two quantities vary in inverse proportion when, as one quantity increases, the other decreases

irrational number a number that cannot be written in the form $\frac{a}{b}$ where a and b are integers

locus (plural: **loci**) the locus of a point is the path taken by the point following a rule or rules

lower bound the bottom limit of a rounded number

mean an average value found by dividing the sum of a set of values by the number of values

median the middle item in an ordered sequence of items

midpoint the point that divides a line into two equal parts

modal class the class with the highest frequency in a grouped frequency table

mode the most frequently occurring value in a data set

multiplier the number by which another number is multiplied

mutually exclusive outcomes two or more outcomes that cannot happen at the same time, e.g. throwing a head and throwing a tail with the same flip of a coin are mutually exclusive events

percentage increase/decrease the change in the proportion or rate per 100 parts

perpendicular bisector a line drawn at right angles to the midpoint of a line

power (also known as **index** or **exponent**) the small digit to the top right of a number that tells you the number of times a number is multiplied by itself, e.g. 5^4 is $5 \times 5 \times 5 \times 5$

plane (figure) a figure or object that lies on a two-dimensional flat surface. Two-dimensional geometry deals with plane figures

polygon a two-dimensional shape that is constructed from a set of three or more straight edges

prime factor a factor that is also a prime number

prime number a number with only two factors: itself and 1

probability tree see **tree diagram**

Pythagoras' theorem the theorem which states that the square of the hypotenuse of a right-angled triangle is equal to the sum of the squares of the other two sides; $a^2 + b^2 = c^2$

quadratic (equation) an equation containing unknowns with maximum power 2, e.g. $y = 2x^2 - 4x + 3$; quadratic equations can have 0, 1 or 2 solutions

quadratic (graph) the graph of a quadratic equation; the curve is smooth and symmetrical

range the spread of data; a single value equal to the difference between the greatest and the least values

ratio the ratio of A to B shows the relative amounts of two or more things and is written without units in its simplest form or in unitary form, e.g. $A : B$ is $5 : 3$ or $A : B$ is $1 : 0.6$

rational number a number that can be written in the form $\frac{a}{b}$ where a and b are integers

reciprocal the reciprocal of any number is 1 divided by the number (the effect of finding the reciprocal of a fraction is to turn it upside down), e.g. the reciprocal of $\frac{2}{3}$ is $\frac{3}{2}$

recurs a repeating pattern; often used when talking about decimals where a digit or string of digits repeats to infinity

reflection a transformation of a shape to give a mirror image of the original

Glossary

regular (polygon) a shape with all the edges of equal length, and all the angles are also equal

relative frequency $=$
$$\frac{\text{Frequency of a particular outcome}}{\text{Total number of trials}}$$

roots in a quadratic equation $ax^2 + bx + c = 0$, the roots are the solutions to the equation

rotation a geometrical transformation in which every point on a figure is turned through the same angle about a given point

scalar a quantity which has only magnitude

scale factor the ratio by which a length or other measurement is increased or decreased

scalene a triangle that has no equal sides or angles

sector a section of a circle between two radii and an arc

set a collection of objects (members)

similar a shape which is an enlargement of another with scale factor $\neq 1$

simple interest interest that accrues only from the initial deposit at the start of each year

simultaneous equations two or more equations that are true at the same time; on a graph, the intersection of two lines or curves is the solution of the simultaneous equations

square number the product of two integers that are equal, e.g. $3^2 = 3 \times 3 = 9$ so 9 is a square number

square root the square root of a is the number that when multiplied by itself (squared) has a result of a

standard form / standard index form a shorthand way of writing very small or very large numbers; these are given in the form $a \times 10^n$, where $1 \leqslant a < 10$

stem and leaf diagram a semi-graphical diagram used for displaying data by splitting the values

subset a set within a set

substitution to exchange or replace, e.g. in a formula

supplementary angles angles that add up to 180°

surd a number written as a square root, e.g. $\sqrt{3}$; a surd is an exact number

tangent a straight line that touches a curve or the circumference of a circle at one point only

term in an expression, any of the quantities connected to each other by an addition or subtraction sign; in a sequence, one of the numbers in the sequence

translation a transformation in which all points of a plane figure are moved by the same amount and in the same direction; the movement can be described by a column vector

tree diagram a way of illustrating outcomes of an event, or combined events; branches are used to show the different outcomes. On a **probability tree**, each branch is labelled with the probability of the outcome for the single event and probabilities are calculated by multiplying along the branches. On a **frequency tree**, the outcomes are shown on the branches and the frequency (number of) outcomes shown at the end of each branch; probabilities can be calculated using the relative frequencies.

trial and improvement a method of solving an equation by making an educated guess and then refining it step-by-step to get a more accurate answer

triangular number an integer that can be represented in a triangle, e.g. the pins in ten-pin bowling: 1, 3, 6, 10, 15, ...

trigonometry the branch of mathematics that shows how to explain and calculate the relationships between the sides and angles of triangles by looking at the ratios of the sides

universal set contains all the objects being discussed

upper bound the top limit of a rounded number

variable an algebraic term which can take different numerical values, generally in relation to a second variable as expressed in an equation

vector a quantity with both magnitude (size) and direction; it can describe a movement on the Cartesian plane using a column, e.g. $\begin{pmatrix} 3 \\ -2 \end{pmatrix}$ which means 3 right and 2 down

Acknowledgements

The authors and publisher are grateful to the copyright holders for permission to use quoted materials and images.

Every effort has been made to trace copyright holders and obtain their permission for the use of copyright material. The authors and publisher will gladly receive information enabling them to rectify any error or omission in subsequent editions. All facts are correct at time of going to press.

Cover and p1 © image Source / Alamy Stock Photo, © Shutterstock.com
All other images are © Shutterstock.com and ©HarperCollins*Publishers*

Published by Collins
An imprint of HarperCollins*Publishers*
1 London Bridge Street
London SE1 9GF

ISBN: 978-0-00-822735-7

First published 2017
10 9 8 7 6 5 4 3 2 1
© HarperCollins*Publishers* Limited 2017

British Library Cataloguing in Publication Data.

A CIP record of this book is available from the British Library.

Commissioning Editors: Katherine Wilkinson and Clare Souza
Authors: Rosie Benton and Jenny Hughes
Editorial: Richard Toms and Amanda Dickson
Proofreading: Alissa McWhinnie
Cover Design: Sarah Duxbury
Inside Concept Design: Paul Oates
Text Design and Layout: QBS Learning
Production: Natalia Rebow
Printed and bound in China by RR Donnelley APS